GOLF COURSE DESIGNS

The beauty of the desert envelops the fifth hole at The Estancia Club in Scottsdale, Arizona. Golfers play over a natural desert area from tees perched on rock outcroppings. Because the natural contour of the ground falls from left to right, the fairway was lifted on the right side and bunkers placed there to balance the strong, rocky features of Pinnacle Peak on the left and to focus play toward the center.

The twelfth at Pablo Creek Club in Jacksonville, Florida is a medium-length par three ringed by trees that plays past a front bunker and a corner of a lake which provides open space amenity for the interior of the course. The marsh plantings along the edge create contrasts of texture and color to the picture

CONTENTS

On Learning

FOREWORD

Glancing through the pages of this book reminds me that I'm fifty-four years old, that I've been designing golf courses for more than thirty-five years, and that the Fazio design imprint is carried by over one hundred and twenty-five golf courses, yet what strikes me most is that I feel we're just starting in this business. I was fortunate in getting an early start in the golf course design business with my uncle, George Fazio, and learning about golf from George and the great masters who were his contemporaries, men like Byron Nelson, Jimmy Demaret, and Sam Snead. As the business and golf grew, I was lucky in my choice of competitors, too, people like Pete Dye, Jack Nicklaus, Arnold Palmer, and many others who became friends, as well as competitors. I've learned from all of them.

I've been lucky in the quality of the men and women who have been attracted to our firm and whose talents as design associates are invaluable to our work; I've learned

---

The rolling terrain at Hartefeld National in eastern Pennsylvania (opposite) provides an unusual setting for a medium-length par five. The fifth hole (looking back from green to fairway) plays over hill and dale, dipping dramatically from a plateau at the landing area that is roughly 275 to 195 yards from the green and continues over a perpendicular hazard that crosses the fairway about 150 yards from the green.

from them, too. As we watch the new generations of golfers perform their magic, we're continuing to learn and, hopefully, we'll be around for quite some time to design more and perhaps better golf courses. Ideally, we would take all that we've learned, put it

with what the industry has learned collectively, mix this knowledge with that of the past, and bring it all into the future. But I have to confess wanting to offer a small apology to past clients because I sometimes feel as though I'm just beginning to know what I'm doing.

We never tried to fool a client about what we could do, and always did the best we could, but I am so much more confident of our abilities now. That seems to come naturally with experience and success, but the truth is that the people and projects described in this book taught us many of our most important lessons. Every one of the golf courses mentioned in this book are special to us. Each story represents a "PhD degree" in golf course design and building. No common approach can be applied to one of these projects. Each presents a new problem requiring a unique solution and a fresh approach that combines past experience, hard work, knowledge, commitment, and, above all, a positive attitude.

When I started in golf design, I remember listening to recognized golf architects and well-known professional golfers talking about "classic" designs, whatever those are, and of building holes styled after the original Redan Hole at North Berwick, the Postage Stamp at Troon, the Road Hole at St. Andrews, and other famous places. And I always had the same reaction to such statements: Why would you want to do something that's already been done? Those are certainly wonderful holes, and stand as historic monuments of the game, but I have no interest in trying to copy them.

We build about six to eight golf courses a year, which means we design a little over one hundred holes each year. They are all different because we look for the differences in each site and each hole. We get no satisfaction in building replicas or copies of holes we've already designed. When people ask me to explain how we manage to come up with different designs, my answer is that I have no idea. We just work at it, and we do it. I've always felt that, no matter what we've done, we can always do it better, and every golf course, every piece of property, every setting is a little bit different. Would an artist want to paint the same picture over and over again? Maybe, but I don't think many would.

Part of our job is to look for the differences, even when the settings are similar. If we can't find a difference, we can create one. That's our job, too. Nature teaches us best. All we have to do is walk the land, open our eyes, and look around to see how many different settings there are in nature, on any site. I've driven down highways and looked out at the terrain and seen great settings for golf holes. I'm sure every golfer has done the same. Anybody that plays golf and loves it has looked over the environment at one time or another and thought, "Wouldn't that make a great golf course?"

In its simplest form, that's really what we do as golf designers. Years ago, there weren't many laws governing golf course design and building. Nowadays, of course, there are more rules to follow. How do you balance drainage issues with environmental constraints, for example? Regardless of the new regulations, site considerations, or other constraints, we still have to get the job done because the only thing that counts is the end result. How good is the golf course? How well does it play? How fair is it? Is it aesthetically pleasing? Nobody wants to hear a story; they just want to play the course and enjoy it. Golf designers can't hide behind excuses because there aren't any. That's as good a motto as any.

Most of the things I have to say in this book are based on common sense and practical experience gained over a period of thirty-five years. The ideas about golf design have been around in one form or another for decades. It's true we have better technology and resources, and a few new rules concerning the environment, but the design concepts and important details are about the same as they were half a century ago. So why publish a book? That's a good question, with a good answer.

The net proceeds from the sale of the book are being donated to The Tom Fazio Charities Fund, which benefits children's charities like the Boys and Girls Clubs of America. My interest in and support of these groups has continued both in my hometown and on a national level for the past two decades because of my belief that there can be no more useful mission than helping the young and underprivileged of America get a start in life. In addition to proceeds from future sales, major contributions to this fund-raising project have come from the golf clubs and golf courses mentioned in the book. My deepest thanks go to all who have contributed.

Tom Fazio

Hendersonville, North Carolina

January 25, 2000

The eighteenth at Forest Creek Golf Club in Pinehurst, North Carolina is shown from the far right side of the

landing area. The fairway slopes right to left, and this hillside bunker directs players toward the left side of the

hole where wetlands and a lake await, a visual distraction on approaches to the green. The sweeping,

curved lines of the bunker edges are a distinguishing design feature at Forest Creek.

GOLF DESIGN TODAY

Golf course design in this country evolved just as the game did, sometimes gradually, sometimes in spurts. People have said all along that power and distance have influenced the game tremendously, and, to a large extent, have dictated the way golf courses were designed. That's true, it has, but I believe economics and advances in construction technology, particularly in the last decade, have had as much influence on golf course design as any physical improvements brought on by better athletes or advances in equipment.

Only in recent years have we learned how to put modern technology to work in the construction of golf courses, and then because clients were willing or determined to commit the necessary resources to their projects. These changes occurred because of competition — other developers began doing it, and golfers themselves began to look for better quality and grander designs.

The tee at the par three seventeenth at Galloway National in New Jersey (opposite) is set on a ridge
to bring the entire hole into view and to offer a panorama of the shoreline and tall buildings of Atlantic City
in the distance. The large bunker structure covering the center and left side makes the hole look harder
than it plays; golfers have ready access to the green on the right.

Golf design today is rooted in the ideals of challenge and aesthetics as much as it ever was, but during the decade of the 1990s it has been driven more and more by grand expectations. The level of expectation grows higher with each project we do, and I'm sure the same is true for other golf designers. Several things may account for this. For one, the golf industry has evolved to the point where a uniform high quality

---

This view of the finishing hole at Pelican Hill's Ocean Course South in California looks back from green to fairway toward the ocean. Golfers must cross a ravine twice to reach the hole (the tee is to the right), hence its name, Double Cross. In this severe topography, we built flat areas for landing areas and greens. The ravine is grassed to help golfers find errant shots and to make the hole playable for the greatest number.

---

exists in the design profession. This talent level is reflected in so many new golf courses by a growing number of well-educated, highly-qualified golf architects. The American Society of Golf Course Architects, co-founded by Donald Ross in 1947, has grown into an organization of about 140 members and, because of this strong talent base, I'm confident design will get even stronger in the future.

For another, information is now spread instantaneously by magazines, newspapers, and the ever-present Internet, which consumes and spits out data almost faster than we can digest it. When a new golf course opens, not only do we hear about it instantly, we see photographs and diagrams of every hole, along with detailed evaluations and criticisms of the design. The mystery of discovering a new golf course for ourselves will never be quite the same.

In short, competition is good and strong, not just among golf designers, but among developers and new clubs to produce the "best" and the "finest" and all the other superlatives. For us, this competition means that to hold a position where clients continue to admire our work and want to hire us, we have to give our total commitment to every single project we undertake. The most important objective we as an organization set for ourselves on every new project is to create a golf course unlike any other we've done before. With the technology and resources available today, that's a realistic and achievable goal. Thirty years ago, I wouldn't have said that. Twenty years ago, I may have believed it was possible; ten years ago, I was just learning how to do it, and now I am convinced it's the only way to go. This evolution is an indication of how much the golf design business has changed.

USING VS. CREATING TERRAIN

Years ago, golf architects would go to a site like The Field Club in Pittsburgh, or Bel-Air in Los Angeles, or Manufacturers Club in Philadelphia that have severe terrain and difficult elevation changes. To lift golfers from a low part of the course to a high spot, elevators were used because no one could imagine trying to tame the site

with technology. Today if we encounter a steep hill or severe elevation, we simply blast and move quantities of rock and earth to create platforms for golf holes and transitions between them.

The same holds true for blind holes, a feature found on mostly older golf courses built in rolling terrain, often with hard, underlying rock formations. No one could suggest a practical reason to change the topography when it would mean great expense, so golf courses were simply laid out along the existing contours of the land. This was accepted procedure around the turn of the century, as can be seen in many golf courses on the eastern seaboard that date from this period. We build courses in the same kind of terrain today by blasting the rock and eliminating blind holes, as we did recently at Hudson National in New York.

Desert environments that previously were difficult or impractical can now be tamed because of improved technology. A flat, uninteresting site in Las Vegas, Ne-

At the fifteenth hole at Hudson National in New York (above) a flurry of bunkers separates the tee-shot landing area from the green, which sits on a ridge beyond one of many granite outcroppings uncovered when rock was removed and slopes were filled and lifted for fairways. Years ago, this would have been a blind hole that played over the rock. A detailed course map of Stock Farm, Hamilton, Montana (opposite), shows the original routing. As often happens when work begins, adjustments are made. Here, we moved the par three tenth to a natural ravine between the twelfth and thirteenth holes and converted the old tenth hole into a practice chipping and short game area. The map also shows how the entry road comes into the heart of the course to expose the region's grand views and open spaces.

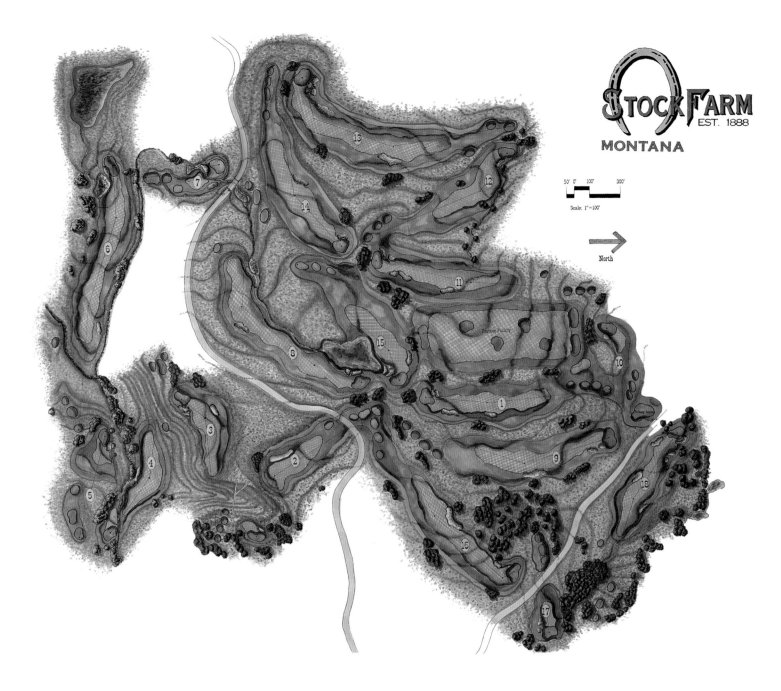

vada barren of any attractive features is formed into a lush, rolling oasis called Shadow Creek, or a gorgeous setting in Scottsdale, Arizona filled with huge boulders is shaped and adapted beautifully to golf, as was done at The Estancia Club. In one case, a golf course was placed in one of the most attractive settings in the world; in the other, a grand setting was created where none existed. Technology allows us to do many things we couldn't have imagined doing two or three decades ago. When designing a golf course in severe, mountain terrain, I think of building the flattest course possible. Of course, the reverse is true when building a course where the terrain is basically flat; there, we want to create contours and hills for relief. But even when designing in difficult country, the end result is what counts. Nobody wants to hear golf designers talk about the problems they encountered, or how tough the site was, or why they had to do one thing instead of another. I remind myself of this every day when tackling difficult terrain.

In the past, the site was the most important thing we looked for in evaluating a project because the land was the key to creating great golf. In the golden age of golf during the 1920s, this was undoubtedly true. But no more. I've heard it said that Tom Fazio only selects good sites and good clients, that he only takes the cream of the crop. Maybe, but only in the sense that, for me, the most important thing in choosing a new project is not the site, but the client. It's important because the golf

course that emerges will be determined as much or more by the client's commitment as it will be by mine, or even by the quality of the raw land.

We look for clients who have a commitment to quality golf. Sometimes we get involved with projects that may never happen, or ones that may not be built for years, as happened with Karsten Creek, the golf course we eventually designed for Mike Holder's golf program at Oklahoma State University. It took Coach Holder almost a decade to find the land and put the deal together, but I was willing to wait. His persistence, his dedication to golf and the people he worked with, and his love for the game impressed me deeply.

A man-made creek guards the approaches to the fifteenth green at Shadow Creek in Las Vegas (opposite).
The rocks forming the gentle cascade were placed by hand. The aerial view of Shadow Creek (above) shows
dramatically the contrast between the original desert and the finished golf course. Here, an unpromising
site was not nearly as important to us as were the client's goals.

The client's commitment made Caves Valley
in the Maryland countryside such an
outstanding place. The par three eighth
plays slightly downhill over tall, weeping
fescues to a green braced by bunkers.

A stately clubhouse forms an attractive backdrop for the approach to the elevated fourth green at Glen Oaks
in West Des Moines, Iowa. The mandate here was to create a world-class golf facility in America's heartland.
The contrast of fine-leafed bent grass fairways and taller, wide-bladed bluegrass rough creates
visual frames on nearly every hole.

I admit to being influenced by a client's attitude toward golf, and toward life. If I'm taken by the concept and believe in the program and if I'm persuaded that a client wants to create great golf, I'm sometimes willing to take a chance that the project may not happen, because I'm interested in the same thing. As for the site, it makes little or no difference whether it's in the flat desert, or on top of a mountain, or at the bottom of a pit because today we have the experience and confidence to create a great golf environment almost anywhere. This is a lesson we're beginning to teach our clients, as well — to expand their thinking and consider the best environment that can be created on their property. There are no secrets to this, just as there are no secrets to designing golf courses. What fits best on a piece of property is a matter of judgment, and it's also a matter of skill and practical imagination. If we can visualize it, we can make it playable, too.

Certainly it's important to understand what clients want before accepting a commission to design a course. If you don't agree with a client's objectives, you probably shouldn't take the job. "The owner wanted it that way," is not an acceptable excuse. Ideally, we should all be designing golf courses based on what we think is best for golf. If we don't believe in designing "the hardest course in the world," or "the easiest to maintain," and can't bring the client around to our way of thinking, we probably ought to pass on the job.

A good number of our projects come about as the result of what I call the "Augusta National Syndrome." It starts when someone who has played Augusta National comes back to their home town and asks, "Why can't my friends and I have a golf course like that?" Some of them can, and actually do; in fact, a few were started by members of Augusta National — Jack Lupton with The Honors Club in Tennessee, Jack Vickers with Castle Pines in Colorado, John Williams with the Golf Club of Oklahoma, Bronson Ingram and Toby Wilt with the Golf Club of Tennessee, and Hall Thompson with Shoal Creek in Alabama are a few examples.

Although many things contributed to this trend, including strong economic conditions, I think the Masters Tournament and its annual awakening of the golf season

on television provided the major stimulus. People were attracted by great stars like Arnold Palmer and Jack Nicklaus, and had dreams about the beautiful golfing terrain at Augusta. Within the past few years, a number of our own clients have built golf courses scaled along similar lines, including Bill Morrow at The Quarry in La Quinta,

---

The eighteenth at Wade Hampton in Cashiers, North Carolina plays straight toward the clubhouse and its wide veranda, giving members a view of the entire hole as they watch golfers finish their rounds. A stream running along the left side of this reachable par five was piped underground in front of the green so that golfers would be allowed to bounce the ball onto the putting surface.

California, Jay Skelton at Pablo Creek in Jacksonville, Bill Conway at Sand Ridge in Cleveland, Andy Hunter and Bob Dayton at Spring Hill in Minneapolis, and Terry Friedman at Victoria National in Evansville, Indiana.

The evolution of the desire to create a special place for golf is really attribut-

---

Short and narrow, the eleventh hole at Karsten Creek in Stillwater, Oklahoma is a blend of design forms. The creek is intimidating but not directly in play unless the pin is on the far left, while the hillside on the right helps balls to bounce back toward the green. Coach Mike Holder was the inspiration for making this one of golf's special places.

able to the game itself and the growing number of people who are attracted to the best features and amenities of the game. We can see how well this sentiment has taken root during the past three or four decades by the way expectations have grown. Each year they become grander and grander. Probably seventy golf courses that fit this high profile have been built over the past few years, and even more are on the drawing boards. In the context of creating golf courses that meet these high expectations, golf designers need more imagination, not less; at the same time, we need less artifice, not more. We do the game a service by resisting temptations to impose artificial solutions on golf designs. If there is a special craft to designing golf holes, it might be a knack for creating proper spaces along the routes of play that encourage enthusiasm and feelings for the game. You may wonder sometimes why you like a golf course? Why does it feel good? Is it just the beauty of the setting, or is it something else? It's hard to pinpoint, sometimes, but part of the reason lies in the shape of a fairway as it traverses the landscape. The actual spaces created for golf and the balance be-

---

Brushy Creek runs the length of the hole and forms the principal hazard at the par four ninth hole at the Golf Club of Tennessee. The creek is also an important visual element and helps balance the space created for golf. The green is elevated above the projected level of a "100-year" flood.

tween those spaces and the visual settings nature provides may be even more important. Golfers respond to these details.

In the Bitterroot Valley near Hamilton, Montana, we recently completed a golf course for Charles Schwab at his Stock Farm property in some of the most spectacular country I've ever seen. Beautiful creeks wind through a valley with purple-tinged mountains rising all around and framing the scene. On a scale of one to ten, the set-

tings around the edges of the golf course are a ten-plus. The golf holes along these edges of the property would be sensational; the interior of the property was not quite so spectacular, but we were not going to settle for anything less. So we turned a possible negative into a positive by clustering golf holes in the interior and creating an environment there that ties in with the surrounding terrain and matches its visual appeal.

The Stock Farm was built eight years after Shadow Creek, the course we carved from the flat, bare desert in Las Vegas. There, at the urging of the client, Steve Wynn, we essentially created a whole environment for the golf course where

---

Usually, we are concerned with fitting holes into smaller frames and spaces, but at the Stock Farm in Montana nature compelled us to think expansively. The par five thirteenth is set against a wide canvas, flanked by white-faced bunkers that mirror the white-capped mountains in the distance.

none had existed. We were very apprehensive about attempting such a massive project, but reluctantly learned that it could be done. The result has been to elevate the expectation levels of both designers and clients. There are no valid reasons to compromise the end product, nor reasons the next golf course shouldn't have as much quality and drama as any we've done. We've gained the experience and confidence to know that, even without good land, we can do what it takes to meet that goal.

Would Donald Ross or Alister Mackenzie be turning in their graves to hear this? No, I don't think so, because they'd be doing the same thing. They would be given the same kind of land and operate under the same constraints and advantages as we do. For them, it would be easy because they were certainly capable men and would have adapted readily to any conditions they found today. This is clear when we examine their courses today and we see how many different environments they tackled and the conditions they worked under. They created quality golf courses wherever they went, perhaps not always, but most of the time.

The biggest difference in the way they worked then as compared with what they would face today relates to the quality of the land. In those days, it didn't make sense to design a golf course on land that was anything other than outstanding because good land for golf was readily available. On the other hand, our technology is so much better today than it was then. In their heyday, Ross and Mackenzie were using mules and scrapers, buggies and scoops, and hand labor. Today, both equipment and financial resources are superior, and I think Ross and MacKenzie would be delighted to take advantage of these advancements. One of our advantages today is that we can

---

A strong finishing hole completes the journey at Pinehurst # 8 (opposite), the Centennial Course at the famous North Carolina resort. Working in Donald Ross' backyard created high expectations. This long par four plays across a natural marsh to a plateau landing area. In keeping with Pinehurst tradition, the green surface rolls off at the sides.

---

see examples of the works of past masters like Ross and Mackenzie, Tillinghast and Flynn. Golf designers can study their courses and decide what they choose to accept as models of good golf course design. Those are our textbooks, our library of golf architecture.

ALTERATIONS VS. ORIGINAL INTENT

This brings us to a debate that has hung around golf for a century or more: Whether or not to modernize, or even touch some of the great old golf courses? Traditionalists argue that the old masterpieces like Pebble Beach and Augusta National should be preserved in as close to their original state as possible. The other side of the argument asserts that there is nothing wrong with updating any golf course, even our most famous designs, because otherwise they would become obsolete and fall into disuse. Golf courses do change whether we like it or not because trees and grass grow, but traditionalists claim that the designer's original intent should not be altered or violated.

Today's golfers might be surprised at how many of the so-called classic golf courses from the 1920s had very little tree cover when they were designed and built. Old photographs of Pine Valley, Augusta National and many other famous courses show that the sites were quite open, yet the golf architect is given credit for designing these courses in a great, wooded setting with the trees in mind. Perhaps

---

A waterfall and the Santa Rosa mountains behind the tenth green (top right) at The Quarry in La Quinta, California lend drama to this par five. The original plans changed when additional land was added well after the design process had commenced. The sixteenth hole at Conway Farms in Lake Forest, Illinois (bottom right) is set in an open field. The ground is shaped to look like natural ridgelines and native grasses are planted on the ridges to provide framing. The fairway doglegs to the left and the flagpole in the distance is a convenient target from the tee.

his intent was to have the trees grow eventually, but perhaps not. Alister Mackenzie and Bobby Jones were not particularly fond of trees too close to the lines of play, and they said so. Yet the one golf course on which they collaborated so famously, the Augusta National, would be almost unrecognizable on television today without the tall trees lining its fairways.

Although it might appeal to our traditional sense if golf courses stayed the same, in practice I don't think this argument holds water, and I'll try to provide an example from one of our recent designs. Galloway National, situated in the same New Jersey pine barrens as Pine Valley, was built in stages because of delays in obtaining environmental approvals. What's more,

the client later acquired additional land on which we eventually built several holes, so the original design obviously changed. People have begun to praise the course, which certainly pleases us, but years from now someone will claim the golf course shouldn't be changed or even touched because nobody should interfere with the

architect's original intent. I would respectfully disagree with that point of view because, in this case, the plan has already been changed once because of the land that was added after the original layout was done.

In reality, a golf course rarely turns out the way a designer originally planned it in

The par four fifteenth, the famous "quarry hole" at Black Diamond in Lecanto, Florida plays from
the rim into the bottom of an old rock quarry. When we started at Black Diamond, we had no idea how the five
holes in the quarry would turn out. They "evolved" as we were building them and were
incorporated into the routing plan.

his mind. Typically, the plan and routing of a golf course evolve throughout the design process to meet conditions and challenges of the site. In some cases, the plan might even be modified to address an environmental issue, a change that usually turns out to benefit the golf course, incidentally. For any number of reasons, what may have been the designer's original intent is subject to regular change and refinement. More to the point, golf courses themselves always change over time. If you compare the photographs, year by year, of Augusta National, Oakmont, and Pine Valley, to take three of the better known golf courses in the United States, you'll notice that the holes as they are today bear only a surface resemblance to their original selves. Bunkers have been moved, replaced, eliminated, and reshaped. Holes have been lengthened or entirely redesigned. Greens have been altered, sometimes beyond recognition. Rough has been grown or removed. Fairways have been widened, edges smoothed, sometimes totally rerouted. Highways have been ploughed through the center of the course. Trees have matured, enclosing a once open golfing landscape. Erosion, drainage, turf disease, modern equipment, convenience, eminent domain seizure by governments, all have had a hand in this evolution.

Personally, I would not put a moustache on the Mona Lisa, nor want to touch any of the old masterpieces of art. But those are inanimate works, fixed in time. Golf courses are organic, living things that change over time. Ask yourself, is the Augusta National of 1999 the same golf course it was in 1939? Is Pebble Beach the same golf course it was when it opened in 1919? You have only to look at the photographs of these golf courses in different decades to realize how much they have changed.

How important is it to preserve a golf course exactly as it was rather than allowing it to evolve with time? Our answers will tell us something about our attitudes toward the game. For me, it is enough to keep the spirit of a golf course intact while keeping it in top condition and in step with the times.

The ninth hole on the Hills Course at Jupiter Hills in Florida is a fascinating one-shotter that plays across

the natural, sandy ground to a sentinel green, a design that was inspired by famed Pine Valley where Uncle

George Fazio once served as the touring professional. This hole was designed several years after

the Hills Course was built when a second course was added.

The eighteenth hole at Old North State Club at Uwharrie Point, North Carolina is a par five "cape hole" that bends ever leftward around the water, and offers many options of how it can be played. Golfers can go directly for the green and the lone guardian bunker, or play safely to the right toward an open bailout area.

A SHORT COURSE AT PINE VALLEY

In one special case, we deliberately set out to build a golf course that not only preserves but copies the images of one of America's grand old courses. The opportunity to build a short course at Pine Valley came rather unexpectedly when the club's chairman, Ernest Ransome, suggested one day that we build a par three course. The club owned several hundred acres adjacent to the famous golf course in what is now the incorporated borough of Pine Valley, New Jersey. The idea startled me. Why, I wondered, would any golf designer want to tackle a project that involves such risk? How would it be received? No matter what was designed, it would be compared with the original course and I could only see a downside to that.

Years ago, my uncle, George Fazio, served as the touring professional at Pine Valley and developed a friendship with John Arthur Brown, then the club's president. Mr. Brown once discussed with him the idea of adding nine holes to Pine Val-

GOLF HOLE COMPARISON ANALYSIS

SHORT COURSE			PINE VALLEY (COMPARABLE HOLE)		
HOLE	YARDAGE RANGE	ELEVATION CHANGE FROM TEE/FWY TO GREEN ORIGINAL FINISH	HOLE	YARDAGE RANGE	ELEVATION CHANGE SHOT TO GREEN *
1	135 - 106	DOWNHILL 27 FT 28 FT	10	146 - 137	DOWNHILL 18 FT
2	178 - 148	DOWNHILL 52 FT 46 FT	14	184 - 168	DOWNHILL 42 FT
3	215 - 106	DOWNHILL 29 FT 29 FT	16	215 - 106	DOWNHILL 20 FT
4	171 - 127	DOWNHILL 6 FT		NO SIMILAR HOLE	
5	342 - 149	UPHILL 28 FT 26 FT	15	342 - 149	UPHILL 27 FT
6	192 - 169	DOWNHILL 38 FT 30 FT	3	181 - 169	DOWNHILL 25 FT
7	227 - 137	DOWNHILL 18 FT 23 FT	13	227 - 137	DOWNHILL 23 FT
8	187 - 94	UPHILL 31 FT 31 FT	17	187 - 94	UPHILL 30 FT
9	166 - 97	DOWNHILL 36 FT		NO SIMILAR HOLE	
10	193 - 83	UPHILL 48 FT 42 FT	2	193 - 83	UPHILL 44 FT
TOTAL	2006 - 1216				

* ELEVATION POINT FOR TEE OR FWY TAKEN FROM LONGEST STARTING POINT.

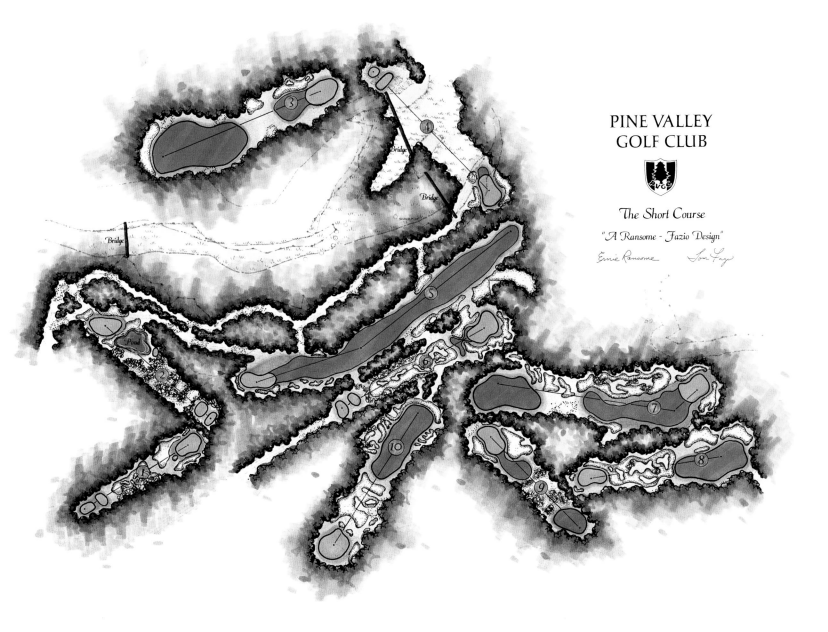

PINE VALLEY
GOLF CLUB

The Short Course
"A Ransome - Fazio Design"
Ernie Ransome   Tom Fazio

ley, which I thought at the time was a bad idea. How could anyone compete with the golf course that's ranked by most experts the best in the United States? So I was not very excited when Ernie Ransome suggested we build a short course. Having been a member at Pine Valley for nearly twenty years, I have developed many good friends there, and it's a place I dearly love. I was very much afraid that if such a project didn't

---

The course map above shows the layout of the Short Course at Pine Valley Golf Club in New Jersey. The fourth and ninth holes are new designs; the rest are replicas of eight famous Pine Valley originals. The chart at left lists the holes and yardages for the Short Course, along with the numbers and yardages of the corresponding holes on the original course.

turn out well, I might never be able to show up again.

Fortunately, Ernie Ransome reassured me that he had no intention of competing with the original course. The main reasons for building a short course were to relieve congestion on the main course and to have a place where members can practice shots on terrain similar to some of Pine Valley's famous holes. The topography chosen was very similar to that encountered by George Crump when he designed the original course in

the years 1912 through 1918, which includes the subsequent completion of Crump's plan by Hugh Wilson in the early 1920s. Unlike those days, however, there were now environmental constraints that might complicate matters. I thought maybe the idea would go away. In the meantime, I agreed to draw some plans.

Three of the holes recreated for the Short Course at Pine Valley are pictured opposite (larger photos) with the originals shown in the adjacent smaller photos. In the top pairing, the sixth hole of the Short Course compares with the third from the original course, a par three that plays from an elevated tee to a cloverleaf-shaped green. In the middle, the tenth hole of the Short Course replicates the second shot into the original second hole, featuring a green partially hidden atop a hill past untended wilderness. The bottom pairing shows the seventh hole of the Short Course from the position of the second shot into the green; this replicates Pine Valley's thirteenth, one of the most famous par fours in golf because of its demand for a first-class long iron shot into the green. The ninth hole on the Short Course (above) is an original design, one of two holes we built to traverse elevation changes between the other holes, and though it does not replicate an existing hole, it captures the Pine Valley look and style.

By this time, both Ransome and I were convinced that Pine Valley should not build a typical par three course, a concept that has been followed successfully at several other golf clubs. Rather, we focused our attention on the shots that seemed

---

The approach to the final hole of the River Course at Kiawah Island Club in South Carolina is both scenic and strong. The hole plays along the edge of a marsh and river framed by massive oaks and dense clusters of palmetto trees. The green is elevated to protect against flooding and ties into a rising grade that leads to the clubhouse on the right.

---

to us the most exciting at Pine Valley. One of my favorite shots is the second to the par four second hole whose green sits like a fortress high above the fairway and is reachable only by a near-perfect iron shot. It's an amazing, exciting, fascinating stroke, and so difficult that if you happen to hit a good shot, you immediately want to hit another. (I should add that when you hit a bad shot, you also want to hit another). Of course, you can't replay shots on the golf course, but wouldn't it be wonderful if you could take a bag of balls and throw them down on a practice fairway that's an exact replica and hit shots to your heart's content?

Other holes golfers would like to play over and over again are the famous thirteenth, and the 600-yard fifteenth, and any of Pine Valley's great par threes — the third, the fifth, the tenth, and the fourteenth. How many victims of the tenth hole, with its diabolical front bunker, have wanted to go back and practice the shot until they were confident they had the hole's measure? As we studied the topographical maps of the adjacent property, we found many of the same elevation changes and features that had shaped these great holes. We started looking for similar terrain to match their settings. Once we started this sort of thing, we were hooked.

We found nearly identical settings at all but one of the par threes, failing only to find one that matched the fifth, and located duplicate second-shot settings for the second, thirteenth, sixteenth, and seventeenth (all par fours), and also the second and third shots for the fifteenth, one of the great par fives in golf. That gave us eight replicas. As we searched for a ninth, Ernie Ransome suggested that, instead, we build two additional holes that would be originals. "No one ever said we had to have a nine-hole course," he said, adding that this would give the club a ten-hole short course enabling members to play a five-hole Nassau. So we designed two new holes, one of which, the fourth, crosses a wetlands where we encountered a pink swamp flower that is on the endangered species list. We decided to build platforms over a part of the habitat so that the plant would not be disturbed.

The plan was submitted to the president, Mel Dickinson, and the Board, and was approved. For construction work, it was decided to use in-house staff, under the supervision of greens superintendent Rick Christian. Because this was such a high-profile course, I didn't think it was fair to assign only one or two of my staff to the project, so almost all of my key people worked on various stages of the design at one time or another. We copied the grades and shaped the greens and bunkers as near to the originals as possible. On some holes we built no tees, which allows members to wander out to a hole and drop balls wherever they wish, including in the bunkers.

Eventually, we put tees on the par three holes. At one, we changed the tee position slightly so that, on a clear day, golfers can actually see the city buildings in Philadelphia twenty miles away. Building the new holes was easier than duplicating the originals; the shapers often jumped off their machines to look at the original holes so they could get a better picture of the fine details, then ran back to shape the new ground.

The club has lately devised special events for the Short Course, as it's now officially known. In the beginning, we did not plan to have tee markers. The idea, according to Ransome, was that whoever won the previous hole earned the privilege of playing the next one from any place he chose. A long hitter might elect to play farther back, while a short hitter might force the match to start closer to the green. This would add an interesting twist to the matches. In another version, the opposing play-

---

The par five ninth at The Farm in Rocky Face, Georgia (top right) plays gradually uphill, bending to the right as it follows a stream flowing along the right side of the hole. Many tales from Civil War days are set in these wooded slopes. At Sand Ridge Golf Club in Chardon, Ohio (middle) we found an intriguing setting for the par three seventeenth. The wide tee provides many angles from which to attack the green. While the right-to-left angle of the green might draw shots toward the dangerous marsh on the left, a generous amount of space is provided on the right side to play safe. The thirteenth at The National in Toronto, Canada (bottom) is a strong par four with a water feature on the left. Rocks were used to create a small cascade, which allowed us to raise the water level near the green so that it's visible from the approach area.

ers would be required to hit the same club on each hole — say, a five iron — but they could place the ball where they wished, wherever they felt most confident of reaching the green with the designated club.

During construction, I remember visiting the site eleven times in a row without giving a thought to hitting a single shot. It was so much fun to go there for a day to help with the shaping of a green or a set of bunkers that I completely forgot about playing the game for a while. Imagine that at a place like Pine Valley! Each time I return, I think back to the worries I had about undertaking this project. Ernie Ransome had as much to do with making it happen as I did and spent many days with rake and shovel refining the greens and other features. That's one of the reasons I refer to it as The Ransome Course.

Being involved in the creation of the Short Course was special to me. It's not even a golf course, as such, and I'm not the designer, in the true sense, but it was a gratifying design experience, and one that I wouldn't have missed for anything.

THE ENVIRONMENT

Environmental issues are now among the most important we encounter in planning and designing golf courses. Thirty years ago or more, the impact of golf courses on the environment was not an issue. Now, conservation is a major concern of people and politics. Fifty years ago, California had a population of twelve million; now it has thirty million. The result of this growth is that conservation of resources has become

much more urgent. Many of the so-called classic golf courses designed in the 1920s and 1930s would not be designed today as they were then because they wouldn't be allowed. Courses are designed differently today not only because of improved equipment, but also because of new rules regarding the environment.

An environmental impact study is required for virtually every new golf project. Meeting the new laws and regulations promulgated by local, regional, state, and federal agencies is part of the design process, and we welcome them, first of all, because it's the law, and secondly, because it makes a lot of sense. It's no good saying we might have routed a golf course or laid out a hole differently if not for the environmental rules. This is no longer a valid excuse. We have learned how to deal with

The par four twelfth at Bayville Golf Club in Virginia Beach plays around the edge of a lake created both for water storage and to obtain earth for shaping contours into the flattish terrain. The "island" tees are set off by native grasses, and the green is elevated several feet above the high-water mark. Bayville is nationally recognized for environmental stewardship.

environmental rules even as they change, like they have over the past fifteen to twenty years.

Because of society's desire to protect the environment, there are many things

---

The Canyons at Bighorn is set in the rugged foothills of the Santa Rosa Mountains in Palm Desert, California. At the second hole, shown here from the right side of the fairway, the idea was to create a memorable feature at the start of the round, so a cascade was built between the tee shot landing area and the green. A major effort was made to protect Bighorn sheep habitat by moving holes and altering the routing.

---

we can't do today that were allowed decades ago. We can't fill wetlands, for example, nor remove trees from certain areas, nor disturb certain kinds of vegetation. We have to design a golf course to play over or around these things. Archeological sites are being recognized and protected more than ever. An example is the seventeenth green of the Ocean Course South at Pelican Hill in Newport Beach, California, where we did the opposite of what we planned. We couldn't excavate a site for the green because excavation would disturb archeological features buried beneath, but we were allowed to place fill on top. Some day, the technology and opportunity may be there

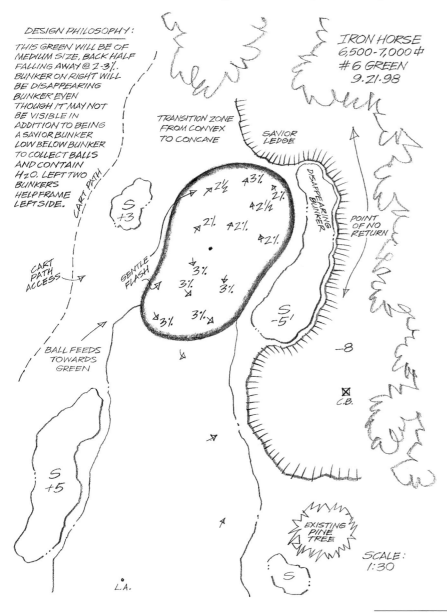

to excavate the site, but, for now, we built the green higher than the existing grade, and I think it actually turned out to be better than the one we originally had planned.

Another example occurred during construction of the Two Rivers Course at Governor's Land in Williamsburg, Virginia, where an archeological site was discovered in the middle of the proposed eighteenth fairway. Once again, we filled and elevated the fairway rather than depress it in order to preserve the site for future generations. At Hudson National north of New York City we found the ruins of an old clubhouse building along the route of the proposed front nine, all that was left of a golf club built in the 1920s but abandoned after a fire and economic setbacks. We decided to design the course around this feature so that golfers could walk among the ruins between the third green and fourth tee, if they wished, as a sort of historical reminder.

Many of the golf courses we're all familiar with probably could not be built today in their present form, or perhaps not at all, because of environmental constraints. For example, many counties have ordinances governing the slopes of terrain; we are not allowed to build on steep slopes, nor even change the grade of an existing slope in many counties. The reason for these ordinances is to protect hillsides and the areas around them. Today, we have to design around these things; years ago, designers were free to incorporate them into the design of the golf course.

Endangered species affect our work much of the time. In Pinehurst, North Carolina, the Red-Cockaded Woodpecker is on a national list of protected species, and we are required to protect their favorite trees. While building Forest Creek and Pinehurst # 8 in the 1990s, we were obliged to leave buffers of at least a hundred feet around

---

The fourth green at Hudson National Golf Club in New York (above) was placed on a plateau beside the ruins of an old clubhouse lost in the 1930s; like environmental considerations, archeological ones increasingly affect design work. The diagram on the opposite page is part of a working drawing for Iron Horse, a recent design at Whitefish, Montana.

---

the trees these woodpeckers use to carve out their nests. Obviously, this affected how and where we routed the golf courses. Twenty years earlier, when we built Pinehurst # 6, we had no such restrictions because the birds were not then on the endangered species list. Besides restrictions placed on the routing, Forest Creek was designed and built using entirely different methods of construction, drainage, and earth works, much of them due to environmental issues.

We went to some lengths to protect nesting birds when building the Belfair West Course near Hilton Head, South Carolina. A large rookery for wood storks and other birds existed in a quiet lagoon along which we planned to build a par three, the eighth, and the tee for the ninth hole. We were not allowed to disturb the birds, which meant that construction could not proceed while the birds were roosting there. We learned when the birds would return to nest, leaving a period of about six weeks in which to build the golf holes. The work was scheduled during that brief window of time, during which we went from raw land to clearing, to earthwork and shaping, green construction and sodding to the finished product, so that all the heavy equipment was gone by the time the birds returned.

I've never had a problem with this kind of effort to protect the environment. In fact, I think it has added character to golf courses in some cases because it preserves habitat for these protected species. In most cases, the natural environment is better than a man-made environment, so the more of it we have, the better golf courses will look.

Surface water drainage is another major issue for golf courses today. Where does the water flow when it rains? What happens to the irrigation water? How far away from wetlands must the golf course be placed? What specific grading contours are

———————————

The ninth hole at Belfair's West Course in the Low Country of South Carolina (opposite) is laid along the edge of a lagoon with clusters of mature oaks framing the green. The large oak on the right is used both as a hazard and a frame for the approach on this par four.

———————

The seventeenth at Two Rivers course at Governor's Land in Williamsburg, Virginia is a dramatic par four that plays along the edge of the St. James River. The wide, flanking bunker is a significant design feature as well as a logical solution to the requirement for an environmental setback separating turf areas from natural waterways. The green is left open at the right side in deference to golfers' instincts to play away from the hazard.

required to preserve the wetlands? How large a detention basin for runoff water will be required? All this, and more, has to be worked out in advance, then approved by local, regional, and state agencies. The old days of walking onto a piece of property, eyeballing the terrain, and dropping a golf hole onto a preferred spot are long gone.

The quarry holes at Black Diamond in Lecanto, Florida have been praised by many golfers for their character and strength, but we're just as proud of how they help to improve the environment. An existing lake within the quarry was protected because it drained into an underground aquifer that is a source of water for the region. During construction, work on erosion control and stormwater management helped redirect surface water from the old quarries into man-made wetlands that filter the runoff. The new wetlands improve water quality and provide needed habitat for fish and wildlife. Abandoned land was reclaimed, and real value was created for both man and the environment. A site once considered of little or no use has become a thriving community that people call their home. In the

---

The par four ninth hole on the Deer Creek course at The Landings opens onto the marsh setting that is one of coastal Georgia's quiet glories, providing a natural environment and background for the green that will never change. We support ideas and programs that protect these kinds of settings.

PETER WONG

larger scale of things, we're as pleased about that as we are of our work on the golf courses.

From the point of view of golf design, wetlands provide contrasts in the color and texture of the vegetation, as well as offering attractive long range views. This tends to add visual and strategic variety to a course, something we look for con-

─────────────

The sixteenth at Spring Hill in Minnesota is a short par five that plays up and across a natural rise to a hilltop green with a grand view of a distant lake. Bunkers set into the slope bridge the steep grade and frame the left side. The green can be reached in two, but only if golfers can carry the ball past a false front on a green that slopes from back to front.

stantly. At Conway Farms near Chicago, we preserved many acres of open wetlands at the northern end of the property, then laid golf holes around them to provide a contrast with the settings on rest of the course, but in a way that does not disturb the natural habitat. There are so many examples of this today; in fact, other than Shadow Creek, it would be hard to name one of our courses where we haven't preserved part of the environment and whose design has not been influenced by it.

In times past, golf designers didn't have to worry about water, or where it went off-site. Now, we not only have to know where to store it, but how it flows, and where it goes. We also must satisfy codes regarding the quality of that water, an issue that relates to the disposition of fertilizers and other substances. In today's world, the water is monitored and analyzed whenever it leaves the property. The industry has become so sophisticated that we often create special subsurface drainage sytems where drainage water can be directed through filter basins to help purify the water.

At the two golf courses we built at Barton Creek in Austin, Texas, major work was undertaken to preserve the water quality of Barton Creek, which is considered one of the pristine creeks in the region. A commitment was made to the environmental agencies and the City of Austin that the golf course would not impact the creek. A

water recirculation system of waterfalls, streams, and holding ponds was constructed to capture water runoff and to filter contaminants, preventing them from reaching the creek. Chemical treatments are not used in any of the water features on the golf courses; in addition, the resort periodically contributes substantial financial resources to long-term environmental improvements.

Close to eighty percent of our projects today have some form of water quality and control system. Someday this technology will be required for all of them. This is not said to be politically correct; I simply believe that it's logical, realistic, and reasonable that we take prudent steps to preserve the environment. Purists may oppose this idea because they don't like to feel they should have to compromise their golfing

The par four thirteenth at Barton Creek's Fazio Canyons Course in Austin, Texas (above) bends left with the terrain. Rock cut from the slope on the right is stacked on the left side to raise the fairway and make it playable, and the exposed wall is retained as a backdrop along the right. The par four second at Pablo Creek in Jacksonville, Florida (top right) plays toward a protected marsh; the frontal bunker is a focal shape alongside the green while adding the texture of sand to the frame of water, trees, and grass. (Middle right) Enough dense vegetation was cleared to leave a strong frame for the downhill, par three fifteenth hole at Hallbrook in Leawood, Kansas. The green was lifted above the creek and angled away from the tee, one of the oldest design principles in golf, and native grasses were planted between tee and green to keep harmony with the natural setting. The ninth at The Virginian (bottom right) is a serpentine par four designed around two natural sink holes on the property, indicated by strong depressions on the right and left. From the landing area, the hole swoops around a sink hole to a green shaped into a hillside beside the shadows on the right.

ideals. Still, there's an element of compromise in life almost every day, and, as inconvenient as environmental rules may seem, we look on them as another challenge to our ingenuity.

They say old dogs don't like to learn new tricks, and humans are no different. Within reason, however, I think learning new rules and new tricks is good for us. If nothing else, it creates more variety, and we can never have too much variety in golf course design to suit me. In the final tally, taking care of the environment provides both the challenge and the opportunity to create better and different types of golf courses.

We have been accustomed to using a certain vocabulary to describe golf courses that dates from the turn of the century. But we're turning a new century this year, and both the practice and vocabulary of golf course design are changing. Many of these differences can be attributed to the new environmental rules that inform us that we can no longer design golf courses as we have in the past. As golf designers, it's up to us to change and to make it work.

MIKE KLEMME/GOLFOTO

A CENTURY OF DESIGN

"I do not know of a single first-class golf course which has been constructed under contract. And it is interesting to note that not a single one of the famous British and American courses have been made in this way."

The words are Alister Mackenzie's, written in 1932 in his final manuscript for a book entitled, *The Spirit of St. Andrews.* The famous golf architect obviously was referring to golf courses built prior to 1932, but his sentiments were honestly felt and point up some of the differences between the practice of golf design then and now. Since Mackenzie's day, many golf courses have been built under fixed-price contracts, although whether he would have considered any of them "first-class" or not, we can only guess.

He goes on to say: "Any contractor who informs a committee that golf courses can be constructed on contract as they would build a clubhouse is either absolutely

———————————

The eighteenth at Victoria National in Indiana is shown from the far left side of the hole, which curls around a lake and finishes at the wide green. The bunker guarding the left side of the green forces shots toward the water. A hard finish to a strong course.

———————

63

ignorant of golf course architecture or is trying to hoodwink the golfing public. It would be just as reasonable to expect an artist to estimate the amount he charges for a painting according to the quantities of paint and materials he uses. It is the mental labour, not the manual labour or materials, which is of paramount importance in any work of art."

I would agree in spirit with what Mackenzie said then, that the artistic touch is needed for the subtle adjustments and details we would want to see in a first-class golf design. But we've come a long way in this profession in seventy years. The artistic touch and the feel for golfing situations will always be needed, but we've learned to make experience, education, and technology work for us in ways Mackenzie and his generation could scarcely have imagined.

Today, we program specific numbers and quantities into each project. We know, for example, that an eighteen hole course will have more or less 140,000 square feet of putting surface. We know that labor and equipment will consume a predictable amount of time and budget. We know much

The contrasting styles of the two golf courses at World Woods in Florida contribute to the concept of a world-class golf destination. The Pine Barrens course (top, the par four fifth hole) is set in open pasture where sprawling, sandy wastes were created to provide the rugged natural look of a pine barrens. (Bottom) The par five third hole is typical of the style on the Rolling Oaks course where bunkers are used to create a more formal, finished look.

The tenth hole at Flint Hills National in Wichita, Kansas plays across a pond that was part of the original ranch. The dense vegetation along the left and behind the green is natural. Multiple tees provide many options for playing the hole, and, while the forced carry goes against our normal design preferences, this was an obvious setting for a distinctive par three.

CHUCK HANEY/IRON HORSE CLUB

The fourteenth green at Iron Horse Golf Club is placed to take advantage of a dramatic setting overlooking the forested areas of central Montana, with a grand view of Whitefish Lake in the distance, a reminder of Mackenzie's admonition to let nature take credit for the work.

more about soil technology and engineering, all of which allows us to proceed, again, in a more orderly and predictable way.

Mackenzie again: "A first-class architect attempts to give the impression that everything has been done by nature and nothing by himself, whereas a contractor tries to make as big a splash as possible and impress committees with the amount of labour and material he has put into the job." In the final analysis, it doesn't matter how much earth you move or how much it costs. What matters is the result, so in that sense Mackenzie was quite right.

In the 1980s, the golf industry found itself building more contours and slopes around the greens to create more interest and comment because clients wanted their golf courses to make the various lists of course rankings. This was also the decade when pressure began to mount to get a golf course ready to play as quickly as possible. Owners didn't want to wait for their new course to mature, so in order to have those steeper slopes and more dramatic contours playable in a shorter period of time, we began laying sod instead of seeding. At first, we put sod on the banks and sides of bunkers, then we began sodding the approaches to the greens, and later on we sodded the steep slopes and difficult drainage areas, anything that might wash away.

Eventually, clients elected to sod entire golf courses, as we did at Shadow Creek and Pelican Hill near the end of the decade. Pelican Hill, located in the arid region of Southern California, would have taken a long time to grow in and the demand for public golf in that area was very high. The client could not open this high profile, high volume golf course with delicate, new turf because the public quickly would have worn out the grass. The only way to achieve mature turf was to sod the entire course, and the cost could be justified by the income generated from greens fees. The decision to sod paid for itself in a fairly short time.

At Shadow Creek, by contrast, there would be very little traffic, but the client wanted to be open for play as soon as possible with a fully mature golf course. So we sodded the course and imported over twenty thousand mature trees and shrubs which were planted on the site. We also sodded the entire course at Champion Hills in my hometown of Hendersonville, North Carolina, but that was done primarily for environmental reasons to prevent erosion.

Different reasons in each case, but the same practical solution. The point is that these measures would never have been contemplated in earlier times because of costs and because there was really no reason for them. There was usually no rush to open a new course because the demand for golf was not as high. Besides, people were more patient in those days. Golf course sites were chosen, for the most part, on reasonable golfing ground where soils were easier to shape and where the terrain did not present great difficulties.

In the so-called "classic" era, designers picked ideal sites whenever possible where golf holes could be easily fit into interesting terrain, but even these ideal sites often had flat or unattractive areas that couldn't be avoided. So designers connected the interesting areas with holes that were not so grand. That's one reason we find a few ordinary holes on some of our most famous courses. Today, we couldn't get away with that. After playing a new course, a golfer might say something like: "Well, it was pretty good, but there were one or two weak holes." In other words, the golfer didn't like one or two holes. The challenge of the 1990s has been to build golf courses that have no weak holes.

The competition among owners and designers to gain instant recognition is probably the principal reason for the current trend toward grander and more dramatic golf courses. So much is written about golf courses and golf design that stories and press accounts now have become part of this competition. In the past, clients were satisfied with, and golfers were content to play, a course that had three or four memorable holes.

In an era driven by drama, there is still a place for classic lines on courses like Forest Creek in Pinehurst, North Carolina. The fifth hole (opposite) is framed by the tall pines, the low vegetation, and graceful slopes indigenous to the region.

Now every new course has to have eighteen "finishing holes," each of which can be the subject of a spectacular photograph for a magazine advertisement or the front cover of a tournament program. Is that a good thing? I won't judge either way, it's just the way things are.

We don't find too many memorable photographic scenes on some of the older, classic designs. Pinehurst # 2, for example, is not dramatic in appearance because it was designed to be played rather than photographed. My photographer friends tell

The eighth at Champion Hills in Hendersonville, North Carolina is a medium-length par four with a bit of drama, playing from an elevated tee over a natural wetland into the heart of the forest to a fairway that slopes gently from left to right. From the tee shot landing area, the hole moves slightly uphill to a plateau green past a lone bunker on the right just short of the target, a dominant and insistent feature.

me it's a hard golf course to photograph, probably because it has so few sharp features or contours. There are no creeks or lakes or waterfalls on Pinehurst # 2, nor strong elevations. Yet it's one of my favorite golf courses and certainly ranks among the best second shot courses in the world. Does that mean the newer courses are overdone? Perhaps some of them are, but I also wonder how high some of the top twenty courses would rank on today's lists if they were brand new and hadn't been designed by a famous architect.

If a golf course with the quality of Pinehurst # 2 were built today, one that had great shot values and design features but little sizzle or flashy eye appeal, would it be well received by golfers and writers and resort owners? The expectations people have today for instant visual impact, the "wow" factor, suggest to me that those days are gone. Golfers want to be thrilled, and they will compare each new

The par three fifth at Galloway National (top) plays across an edge of marsh on the Jersey shore and is an example of using very little land to create a golf hole; both tee and green sit on slivers of high ground on pieces of a peninsula. The par five tenth at Old Overton in Alabama (bottom) plays along a ridgetop to a small green set into the backslope of a hill, surrounded by contours and bunkers designed to save as many shots as they punish.

Drama and color drench this par three, the downhill thirteenth at Maroon Creek in Colorado, framed by the creek on the left and colorful aspen everywhere with the slopes of the Highland skiing area rising in the background.

DICK DURRANCE II

course with the best they have played before. Golfers and owners alike want instant gratification. A phrase we hear a lot today is the "Now Generation," and it's as applicable to golf course design as to anything else in our culture.

Even when golf designers are given a poor piece of land or a low budget, clients and golfers alike expect them to create something special. When a brand new golf course opens today it's compared immediately with the classic courses and judged accordingly. But when those same classic courses opened years ago, they were not judged in the same way. Even those that were highly touted were given time to mature because everyone understood that a golf course needed a number of years to settle in, for the vegetation to fill

---

The eighth hole at Butler National in Chicago (above) was built along a rim of a creek because the existing grades and a history of flooding along Salt Creek made it impractical to place anything but a par three on this part of the property. Tees and green were shaped on the top of a "dam" while the rock facings along the edge of the water protect against floods. The tenth hole at The Farm in Rocky Face, Georgia (top right), is a shortish par four cut straight into a wooded hillside. The fairway was made by cutting on the left and filling on the right to create a level playing surface. Shadows from the dense forest on the left give the illusion that the hole is longer than it is. The eighteenth at Dancing Rabbit's Azaleas Course (bottom right) follows the site's rolling terrain into a green slightly angled to the line of play beside a lake that is shaped into its right side. The clubhouse with its multiple porches is an attractive backdrop and vantage point for those watching golfers finish.

out, and for its architectural features to be adjusted and refined.

Not many golfers today would be satisfied with an immature course. A developer would have a hard time selling memberships or greens fees at such a course. Golfers want a quality experience, and have very little interest in the engineering problems the designer may have encountered or whether it was a good site or a poor site. As I said earlier, none of that matters. I doubt that we'll go back to doing things the way we've done them in the past. We now have brand new courses where we never dreamed golf courses might exist and great courses in a few states that thirty years ago didn't have a quality golf course. If anything, golf course design is just beginning.

A NEW TECHNOLOGY

Technically, we're capable of doing so much more than the classic architects were. Many of the things done by Donald Ross or A. W. Tillinghast or William Flynn were dictated by the limitations of machinery and construction methods. Their design decisions might fairly be described as "rub of the green," rather than rub of the designer's pen, because they didn't have the equipment to do otherwise. Nature made the decision for them. In my opinion, we never want to get away from the old tenets of course design, but we're dealing with entirely different capabilities than the "classic" architects were.

Few of the great, old courses had drainage pipes. In fact, storm drainage was not a part of course design. Everything surface drained. Floods came and were tolerated. People waited for the water to run off. Even thirty years ago, we didn't excavate a big hole in the ground because we would have had to install an expensive pipe and provide for drainage. Today we must design detention systems that will hold flood water on the property. It's the law in most places. With the technology available now, we only need to know "how deep should we dig?" If the water table is too high, or too low, we have plenty of pipe and strong pumps to handle the flow of water.

At Butler National in Chicago, for example, we designed the par three eighth along a curve of Salt Creek. However, the intended fairway was actually lower than

---

The par four eleventh hole on the Cypress Course at Bonita Bay East near Naples, Florida (opposite) is an example of using modern construction techniques to minimize or altogether avoid environmental impacts.

the creek. We simply built a little berm and rerouted the water through the desired creek bed; the water is pumped uphill and over the berm to Salt Creek. Pipes and pumps are not always needed for good storm drainage. By contrast, when we built Galloway National along the edge of the bay across from Atlantic City, New Jersey, we reshaped the site itself. Environmental regulations do not permit surface water to run into nearby Reed's Bay because it's a protected habitat. However, the interior of the Galloway National property is sandy loam soil, which is permeable, so we were able to easily create depressions and contours — which fit perfectly with the design

---

Photos on these two pages show rocks used in different settings to protect golf holes. At the par three eleventh at Conway Farms in Illinois (above left), rocks placed on a slope above the lake prevent erosion from choppy waves created by strong winds in this suburb of the Windy City. In Greenville, South Carolina (above right), the par four opening hole at Thornblade plays from an elevated tee across Brushy Creek where a rocky wall was built to guard the fairway against flash floods.

concept of the course — that now helps retain flood water on site until it percolates through the sand to the water table below.

Could Ross or Tillinghast have done that? Of course they could, with modern training and experience, maybe as well as or better than anyone. They were certainly able to do outstanding work on wonderful pieces of ground, even on land that wasn't so wonderful, and produce interesting, lasting work. But they also did some things that today wouldn't be acceptable. Some of the holes on our famous golf courses, even some designed by legendary designers, wouldn't pass muster with

----

At Emerald Dunes in West Palm Beach, Florida (above left), rocks excavated from the site support a fortress green above the lake at the par three sixteenth, a hole designed with an aquatic flavor in keeping with the environment of the site. (Above right) Barton Creek's Fazio Foothills Course is set in the rugged terrain near Austin, Texas where rocks are used to buttress the ninth green and the wall of the back bunker, a hole chosen among the best eighteen modern designs by golf writer Dan Jenkins.

today's golfers. Back then, you didn't blast away a pile of rock to remove a blind spot; you just played over it. It was an issue of economics and equipment. If we tried that today, we'd be run out of town because golfers don't like blind holes and it's easy to avoid building them. In fact, we now have experts who can drill into rock in a certain way and blast huge boulders into any size rock we want. We can then take the sized-to-order rocks and build a stone wall in front of a green or tee. We've done that at Barton Creek in Texas and Hallbrook in Kansas City and many other places.

Another significant difference is the impact of environmental rules on design issues. Many of the great golf holes on famous courses could not be built today because of new laws that protect the environment. The seventh hole at Pebble Beach, for example, is one of the famous par threes in America even though it measures only 110 yards and plays downhill. It hangs on the edge of a headland above the Pacific

The par three seventeenth at Deer Creek in Savannah (above) is frequently bathed in shadows; the "weeping" Live Oaks towering on the right provide a visual counter-weight to the flat, open marsh in the distance. (Opposite) White Columns, designed as a high-profile public fee course in 1994, finishes alongside a lake in gently rolling terrain in Atlanta. It has become one of the most successful public courses in America.

The eighteenth at Johns Island West in Florida (above) takes advantage of natural sand ridges that provide

perches for the tee, the clubhouse, and the final green. The contours are most unusual for Florida. The large volume

of play at Pelican Hill in California (opposite) dictated multiple pin positions at the par three thirteenth on the

resort's Ocean Course South; instead of building one large green, however, two smaller ones were created

to better capture the drama along the ocean edge.

Ocean, and golfers can almost putt the ball onto the green from the tee; but when the wind blows, it can take a full three iron to reach the flag. Today, you might be able to build a golf course on the Pebble Beach site along the edge of the ocean, but maybe not that hole because of rules requiring setbacks from cliffs and other sensitive coastal areas.

At the turn of the century and even up until the 1950s, if an architect came across a swamp, he was free to drain and fill it. Part of the land on the southern border of Seminole Golf Club built in 1930 in Florida, for example, was a low area that was filled to complete the last three holes of the front nine along the entry road. Today that method of construction would not be allowed. The eleventh hole on the East Course at Merion in Philadelphia is one of the most famous in golf; it was on that green that Bobby Jones closed out his match with Gene Homans to win the U. S. Amateur title in 1930 and clinch his famous Grand Slam. The triangular green on this historic par four sits behind a fork in Cobbs Creek on a low point of the property, a wonderful setting framed by stately trees. It was a natural, strategic gem when golf architect Hugh Wilson found it there at the edge of the property in 1912, but one that probably would not be allowed today in its exact location due to environmental constraints of the site.

Those days are no more. Today we must leave wetlands as we find them, and in some cases stay fifty or a hundred feet away from the edge, depending upon local rules. We deal with that today by turning a negative into a positive, by creating great backdrops for golf, or what my uncle, George Fazio, called "the outside influence."

At Pinehurst # 8, which was built in 1996, not only did we preserve swamps and wetlands, we created additional wetlands to enhance the aesthetic surroundings. This was also a major issue in the design of Bonita Bay East in Naples, Florida, whose continuing efforts in environmental conservation have earned special recognition from the Audubon Sanctuary Program.

Another difference between yesterday and today is the demand for outstanding practice facilities. How many of America's famous golf courses were built without practice ranges? Pine Valley, Merion, Cypress Point, Pebble Beach, Seminole, Augusta National, and most public courses were all designed and built without a formal practice facility because, in those days, golfers were allowed to practice on the golf course itself. Or, at places like Seminole and Augusta National, spaces between holes were used for practice.

Can anyone imagine a new golf course

The seventh at Hallbrook in Kansas (top) plays into a small valley and across a creek that divides the fairway near the green. This par four plays from high right to low left but the green is shaped from high left to low right, a deliberate design treatment so golfers can play on both sides of the slope. (Bottom) The approach to the tenth green at the Old North State Club in North Carolina is shown from the left side. By extending the natural high ground from the right, we were able to form the green on level ground and create the cavern bunker on the left.

This aerial photo shows the placement of back-to-back par threes, the eleventh in the foreground and the fourteenth beyond, on the Hills Course at Jupiter Hills in Tequesta, Florida, both of which play down from a single tall dune in opposite directions to greens guarded by water. This arrangement is designed to take maximum advantage of prevailing winds off the nearby ocean.

today without a first-class practice area? Golfers in the twenties and thirties didn't practice as much as they do now. Now we build world-class practice facilities everywhere, including at public golf courses, with tees as deep as they are wide and capable of accommodating forty or fifty people at a time. Golfers want more than a place to warm up before the round starts; they want a place to work on their games after play is done, just as the professionals do.

Because of the enormous influence of real estate on the development of new golf courses over the past few decades, it has become fashionable for golfers and writers to criticize any intrusion of housing onto golf courses. None of us wants to see that happen, although the critics seem to suggest that golf must be kept far from real estate. The purists might want to remember that many of America's most famous golf courses have housing: Pebble Beach, Riviera, Pinehurst # 2, Winged Foot, Cypress Point, and Pine Valley, all have houses along some of the fairways. Just because a golf course has homes alongside the holes doesn't necessarily mean it's bad.

The sixth at Reynolds National in Georgia (above) is a short par five that plays downhill along the edge of a ravine to a peninsula green jutting into the lake. White bunkers contrast with the dense shaded areas along the right side and provide a buffer between fairway and ravine. The opening hole at Bayville in Virginia Beach (opposite) establishes two of the design treatments used on this open site: the rolling contours and free-form bunker styles of links golf.

If we were to design a course like Royal Portrush, for example, we'd probably be criticized because a golfer's first view on the very first tee takes in a large trailer park, yet it's one of the world's great courses. Of course, Royal Portrush is in Ireland, in a resort area where people come in summertime to be close to the sea, so the trailer park is accepted. But if we built something like this today in Indiana or Pennsylvania, golfers would complain: "Look at that awful view. How could anyone put a golf course there?" I

certainly wouldn't disagree with that, and it just points up one of the many differences between designing golf courses now versus fifty or a hundred years ago.

THE TWO GOLDEN AGES

Golf historians have described the 1920s as "the Golden Age of Golf Course Design" in part because so many new golf courses were built during the decade leading up to the Great Depression. The stock market crash and the long economic bust that followed brought a virtual halt to golf course construction, an interruption that continued until the end of World War II and through the late 1940s. In fact, golf course design has followed the economic times pretty closely for the past hundred years. The decade of the 1990s has been a watershed for golf design because of the strength and health of the economy. We can mark it down as a given that the current economic conditions have had a tremendous effect on the industry. There are more

The thirteenth hole on the Ranch Course at Black Diamond in Florida (above) is framed by long bunker shapes and clusters of mature oaks and pines, showing a marked contrast with its more famous sibling, the Quarry Course. The fourteenth hole on the Desert Course (top right) at The Vintage Club in Indian Wells, California is set into a grove of Palo Verde trees found on the site. While different from any other setting on the course, the grove was not removed; instead, a par three was created around and through the trees that offers its own natural and distinctive beauty. The par three sixth at Glen Oaks in Iowa (bottom right) plays downhill to a green shaped nicely into a large pond and framed by a catch bunker left and a flash bunker right. The high tee allows golfers to take in the long range views of Iowa's beautiful rolling terrain, dispelling notions that the prairie is always flat.

and better golf designers than ever in our history, and they're building better products now than have ever been built before.

I can't imagine designing a golf course today that didn't have proper greens construction, careful site engineering, efficient storm drainage, automatic irrigation, attractive landscaping and other things that we now take for granted. These are major differences in design craft since I began work in the mid-1960s. The cost is much different, too, but look at the cars we drive today. Even a mid-priced automobile has standard features like seat belts, fuel injection, automatic transmission, radios, air bags, safety tires, air conditioning, and so forth. All these things add to the cost. Should we have them? Of course, we should; we have every reason to expect improved safety and performance in our automobiles. We wouldn't accept one without these features.

The same is true of golf courses, and the same will be true fifty years or a hundred years from now. Our knowledge and skills will be better, our machines and tech-

niques more efficient, our experience and confidence in dealing with difficult problems that much greater. We can see this working already. America's newest golf courses, those opened in the last decade, are as good as any ever built, in my opinion. They were designed to a higher standard than their predecessors, and the competition among owners and developers is stronger than it has ever been. All of this contributes to a better product.

We say that the courses built in the 1920s are "classics" because they have so much history associated with them and many of the legendary players have left their

legacies there. But "the old days" are different for everyone. For me, the old days were the 1960s. For Robert Trent Jones, the old days may have been the 1920s. For someone else, the old days are the 1980s, and for another person the old, classic days will be the 1990s. Here's a statement the pundits can chew on: When we look back at the last decade of the twentieth century, I am reasonably confident that it will be remembered as its own golden age of golf course design. To be even bolder, I'll suggest that when the experts later this century look back and assess the past

hundred years of golf architecture, their rankings will indicate that a majority of the premier courses of the twentieth century were designed in the 1990s.

In this business, as in so many others, a golf designer is only as good as what he or she has done lately. With the proliferation of media coverage and the demand to be included in the various golf course rankings, we must pay attention to every small detail of every hole we design. This translates into our expectations for ourselves and the performance levels we expect from our staffs. And why shouldn't we do it better now than we did a decade ago, or even a year ago? There's no reason at all. We're judged on what we've done in the past, and it's nice to receive recognition from

The third hole at The Quarry in La Quinta, California (above) plays along a plateau beside the open

desert and serves as a "rung" to climb to higher elevations of the property. The tee is elevated to give

golfers a clear view of the shape of the hole and the hazards waiting down the left side. A lagoon snakes

through the thirteenth at Kiawah Island Club's River Course (opposite) providing the principle hazard

and fascination on this long par five. The water crosses the fairway beyond the tee shot landing

area and from there stays on the right side all the way to the green.

golfers and clients. But I prefer to look ahead to the next project because of my strong belief that the next course will be the best one.

COURSE RANKINGS

The United States Golf Association began rating golf courses as part of its handicap system. This system is designed to provide golfers with a fair method of comparing the skill of one golfer to another, from one golf course to another. The course rating system was largely based on a mathematical formula in which officials assigned numerical ratings to various components of a golf course, like length, width, hazards, difficulty of greens, and so forth. In this scheme, length was assigned more weight than other factors. The fact is, golfers and pundits have been compiling their own lists of "great" or "best" golf courses for a hundred years or more.

In the late 1960s, *Golf Digest* published a list, based on the USGA numerical ratings, that it called the "200 Toughest Golf Courses in America." Then, in 1969, the magazine published a new list, reducing the number to 100 courses and imposing its own criteria for selection based partly on a newer USGA evaluation system and partly on the judgment of leading pros and amateurs in each region of the country rather than on the old numerical formula. This list of "America's 100 Greatest Tests of Golf" was a big hit, and has been revised and reissued every two years. Soon, every magazine worth its name was publishing a list of "great courses," and today the demand to be included has almost overwhelmed publishers' capacity, but not readers' interest.

It shouldn't surprise anyone that this publishing and marketing bonanza created

The short par four tenth (top right) plays through a narrow corridor of trees, setting the tone for the back nine at Caves Valley in Owings Mills, Maryland. Aspens frame the fourteenth hole at Maroon Creek in Colorado (middle right) providing brilliant contrasts with the turf. The seventeenth at Edgewood Tahoe in Nevada (bottom right) plays along Lake Tahoe's beach beneath massive Ponderosa pines, a grand setting for this par three.

a tremendous interest in golf design, and that it also created some mischief. Here's something we might consider: If roughly five thousand courses have been built since 1975, how many of them belong on a list of the best one hundred? That's not an easy question to answer, but it's a fair guess that somewhere between fifty and seventy-five courses built in the period 1992 to 1999 would fit the profile of quality and excellence the raters look for in honoring golf design. In fact, you wouldn't be far wrong in thinking that maybe five hundred golf courses built since 1975 would fairly qualify. Maybe a thousand. One magazine actually rates the hundred best courses built prior to 1960, and the hundred best built since. That seems to me a much fairer approach to a nearly impossible task.

Back in the 1960s, a golfwriter or panelist would play a new golf course and say after finishing the round: "Some day when that course matures, it has a chance to be good." That was the best a designer could hope for, a sign that the job had been well done. Today, that reaction would signal a failure! Nowadays it's unnecessary to wait while a course matures.

The sixteenth at Wild Dunes in South Carolina (above) plays across the edge of a marsh toward the inland waterway. The small pocket bunkers at the green and the long views over the water hint at a links setting which is fulfilled on the two holes that follow. The contrasts at Long Point on Amelia Island, Florida (opposite) can be seen at the fifteenth (top right) and third (bottom right) holes. The fifteenth is a short par three along the shore, while the third is a longer one-shotter set among the pines, palms, and magnolias of the interior holes.

No need to wait for small seedlings to grow into big trees; plant big ones. Plant mature sod on the steep slopes and faces of bunkers; even better, sod the entire golf course and be ready for play in a few weeks. Choose an environment, if you like, perhaps a creek, a waterfall, a severe elevation and place it where you will. Whether we like it or not, this is the new paradigm.

Those who accept the responsibility to rate golf courses are sometimes chosen for reasons other than playing skill or a familiarity with golf architecture, and are guided by criteria set by the rating organization. It's also true, or at least we hope it is, that their selections and votes are based on the golf courses they know. What of those they don't know? The quality of "greatness" is a measure of what people say about a golf course. In the end, we know that the choices are based as much on popularity and personal opinion as on objective judgment. As we've seen, a golfer can't very well measure a course with a ruler if he wants to discover its quality.

Over time, the opinions of knowledgeable golfers have determined the reputation of a golf course, and a consensus gradually emerges. This custom is both good and bad. Good because it represents the judgment of a large number of golfers from different generations who have had time to evaluate a particular golf course. Bad because the judg-

ments are often colored by historical events that have taken place on these courses and because custom is slow to recognize change.

Since *Golf Digest*'s first poll in 1966, an average of one to two hundred golf courses a year have been built. That's about 5,000 to 6,000 courses, but since only the top hundred are ranked, "classic" courses still dominate the rankings. Should they? They probably should. Tradition is an important part of the game, and I think all of us feel that the golf courses we've loved and cherished so long should not be dropped from the lists. At the same time, I have a feeling that there are probably a thousand to fifteen hundred golf courses that deserve to be ranked among the top hundred because they

---

The par four sixteenth at Galloway National across the bay from Atlantic City, New Jersey blends textures of turf, sand, water, and dense vegetation with enough golfing interest to tempt both the mighty and the meek. Most of the trouble is on the left to catch errant draws and hooks by better golfers while leaving the rest of us to contend with a bushy clump of trees crowding in on the right.

are equal in quality to those that are ranked. Some of the new ones are as good as any golf course ever done but don't get "ranked" as high. I expect that popularity has a lot to do with it, but I guess that's human nature.

Perhaps it might be worth experimenting with some sort of trial period in which the new golf courses would go on a waiting list. On the other hand, the polls are wonderful for golf and they've certainly been very generous to me. They create controversy and interest, and are a positive influence. I suppose if the magazines doubled the number of courses on the lists it might dilute their impact, but I wish the various publications could find a way to recognize a few more golf courses, both

---

The rolling contours of the eighteenth fairway at The Virginian, caused by natural sinkholes on the property, are combined with small bunker clusters along the right and the deep depression in front of the green to produce a strong finishing hole. The big oak to the right of the green was an obvious landmark for the green, whose contours were shaped just outside the drip-line of the tree.

classic and modern. There are so many that seem deserving.

As I mentioned earlier, a number of famous courses have enjoyed high ranking and reputation in part because of historic events associated with their names, but I'm not sure all of these courses could stand up against some of today's courses. The industry today is building better courses, and there is a deep pool of talented young people in the profession, a group that is probably as gifted and able as any generation of designers in golf's history. I feel very fortunate that some of them have chosen to work on our design team, where they continue to contribute their talents and insights.

GOLF DESIGN THROUGH THE ERAS

Golf began in the United States a little more than one hundred years ago. In the relatively short span of time since then, golf has changed and grown enormously.

The third green at Ventana Canyon in Tucson, Arizona (above) seems to teeter between jagged boulders, a tiny hole of just a hundred yards and, yard for yard, one of the most expensive we've ever built. (Top right) The dogleg sixteenth is one of the few holes where golfers have a chance of avoiding trouble at The National Golf Club in Toronto, Canada. What deceives golfers is that no bunkers are placed in front of the green, so judging distance is the biggest challenge. The fifth at Butler National in Chicago (middle right) presents a large, peninsula green with several levels and, no matter where the pin, a long carry over water. A difficult par three. (Bottom right) Bunkers on the left and right set up the strategy on the sixth hole at Black Diamond in Florida. In addition, the tall pine on the left, the safest side, tends to force golfers to the more dangerous right side.

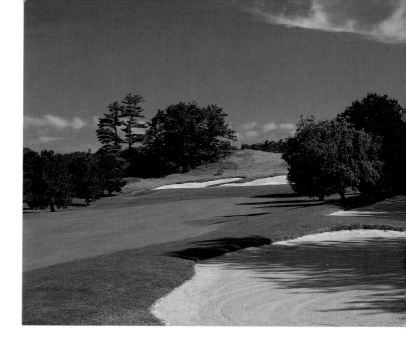

It has gone through three or four major booms in popularity, the latest of which is still going on and is undoubtedly its greatest. The first took its impetus from the post-Civil War industrialization and economic expansion that peaked in the 1880s, a period that Mark Twain dubbed "The Gilded Age." From a few dozen golf courses in the early 1890s, the game has spread throughout the land and grown to more than sixteen thousand courses. Changes in equipment led to major changes in the way the game was played and the way golf courses were built. The style of golf evolved by the game's heroes in response to these changes is an interesting and fairly accurate mirror of the way conditions have affected golf over the decades, from Francis Ouimet to Bobby Jones to Ben Hogan to Arnold Palmer to Jack Nicklaus and, today, to Tiger Woods and his generation.

Golf was one of several crazes that received a significant boost from the economic boom of the 1920s, and this undoubtedly contributed to the decades's reputation as the golden age of golf architecture. Scottish designers like Donald Ross and Alister Mackenzie came to the fore during

this era which coincided with the rise of an extraordinary group of American architects that included A. W. Tillinghast, George Thomas, William Flynn, and amateur designers George Crump and Hugh Wilson, all of whom coincidentally began in Philadelphia. This period marked the flowering of a distinctly American look in golf, heavily influenced by the parkland settings of a majority of the sites these men were given but also displaying a surprising range of individuality and styles.

During the economic depression of the thirties and continuing through the Second World War, golf architecture went through a long decline. In fact, many courses were lost to military installations and foreclosures. When the post-war economy perked up, so did the golf design business. Men like Robert Trent Jones, a self-starter and man of unlimited energy, and Dick Wilson, a disciple of Hugh Wilson and Bill Flynn, led the way in this new wave of course building that coincided with major growth in population and golf. More people were moving to the suburbs, more suburbs were being built, more people were playing golf, and more courses were being built. When Dwight D. Eisenhower became president in 1952, the boom gained momentum, and when Arnold Palmer came on the scene shortly thereafter, it acquired a full head of steam.

By this time, television was starting to make inroads in golf, showing the major championships and some of the other attractive tournaments, but the networks only showed the last four holes. As a result, we noticed that clients in the sixties frequently put an emphasis on the design of the last four holes, either citing public relations reasons or hoping to snare a televised golf event. In order for the golf course to be memorable, a designer usually wanted those last few holes to be impressive.

Then came the polls and golf course rankings, which were discussed earlier. These gave rise to the term, "Signature Hole," which, in my opinion, is a dreadful and sad cliche that probably has done as much harm as any phrase I can recall. When I'm asked what signature holes I've designed, I never know what to say. A signature of what, I'm tempted to reply? One fellow asked me what signature *courses* I have

designed. That stumped me completely. They're all signature golf courses, I suppose, because they are individual. Is that the right answer?

Automatic irrigation came into vogue during the seventies, a major change because now we could irrigate wider areas and courses began to look greener. "Long" was "in," and courses of 7,000-plus yards became common. This decade of "long and

---

A series of tees along Brushy Creek sets up a stout driving hole at the eighteenth of the Golf Club of Tennessee. The creek flows in front of the tee down the entire left side of the fairway, which bends slightly to the left and finishes beside the clubhouse.

strong" was due, in part, to the increasing visibility of the professional tour on television and to the fact that a growing number of tour players had decided to get into the golf design business. Developers were eager to claim their golf course was strongest of all, and length mattered.

We, too, built long courses. Jupiter Hills and Butler National were designed at about 7,250 yards, and Pinehurst # 6, also designed by us during this era, was even longer. In the designer's defense, the intent never was to play these courses at 7,200 yards, but rather to provide maximum flexibility to adjust the course based on daily conditions of wind, tee, and pin placements. On this basis, you might never play these "long and strong" courses at more than 6,800 or 6,900 yards.

This period was followed by a small recession that led some designers to build courses that required less wall-to-wall maintenance. Natural areas were left as hazards and aesthetic complements that needed no tending, and therefore saved money. My good friend, Pete Dye, was the leader of this movement, and he produced a number

---

Golfers aim at the flagpole on the finishing hole at Conway Farms in Lake Forest, Illinois (opposite) and must thread their way safely past a serpentine creek that crosses the fairway near the landing area and then travels down the left side before crossing again in front of the green. The approach to the eighth at Grayhawk's Raptor Course in Scottsdale, Arizona (above) shows how movement is created on a relatively flat piece of ground by carving undulations into it and thereby lifting bunkers and greens while lowering the surrounding elevations.

STEPHEN SZURLEJ

The par three sixteenth at Victoria National in Indiana is shown looking back from the green to multiple tees set on rugged spoil areas between two lakes created by an earlier mining operation. The lakes are connected by a stream flowing downhill from one to another, and the green is reached over the walker's bridge on left. The fifteenth hole, to the right of the upper lake, is a par five that plays to the distant green.

of wonderful golf courses following this approach. A reaction to the long, hard courses that had been influenced by the pros set in near the end of the decade as the industry began to realize that long was not necessarily great. We ourselves turned the corner in 1979 and 1980 with the design of Wild Dunes in South Carolina and The Vintage Club in Palm Springs, California, both of which were well under 7,000 yards in length. In both cases, we knew they didn't need to be long to be good tests or to carry an image of quality. We felt we were bucking a trend at the time, and I think others did, too.

Boom times returned in the early eighties, and everyone wanted more golf courses. The competition to earn a spot among the course ratings was building; a resort or hotel course that ranked higher might sell more hotel rooms; a private residential develop-

The twelfth hole at Deer Creek at The Landings in Georgia (top) is a medium length par three whose green is guarded by steep, shadowy contours surrounded by the dense pine forest of the coastal plain. The seventh at Thornblade in Greenville, South Carolina (bottom) is a short par four playing over a creek with small pot bunkers placed on the far slope to keep balls from running down into the water.

ment with a highly rated course might attract more buyers. If water, sand, creeks, and waterfalls were good, then having more of them must be better. The industry kept doing more and more — more elevation, more water, more drama, more bumps, more of everything. Instead of having four great holes at the end of the course, now every hole had to be a "finishing hole." This made for some very difficult golf courses.

What would be next? A change in the tax laws in 1986 put a damper on construction and real estate development which slowed golf course building for several years. Meanwhile, the industry went back to a style resembling that of the older, classic courses. To be considered good, or even great, a golf course no longer needed to be long and difficult, the critics said. New awards were announced by golf publications for "Best New Golf Courses of the Year," and we were off on another race.

This led us into the nineties and the emergence of greater drama with an emphasis on beauty and visual impact, a kind of rebellion against the hard courses of the eighties. In the nineties, contours actually became softer and gentler, not more se-

---

The thirteenth green at Flint Hills National in Wichita, Kansas (above) is shaped with classic noses leading to and from bunkers and feeding into the green itself. Native grasses on the left and the rich curtain of vegetation in back complete the frame. The third at Old Overton in Birmingham, Alabama (opposite) is a short but dramatic par three that almost seems to drop from under golfers' feet. A steep bunker on the left might cause second thoughts while aiming.

vere. The term "minimalism" was coined during this time by those who felt that there had been an excessive amount of earth-moving in the previous decade, driven by some of the more exotic designs, and declared a need to return to an earlier, simpler model of course design.

A hundred years ago, golf was played along the ground, as it still is in Britain, for the most part. In America, the industry transformed golf into a game played in the air. Clients desired ever-lusher, dark green turf, and consequently bigger irrigation

systems and pumped greater quantities of water. Turf became softer so golfers had to play more through the air because they could no longer bounce the ball into the greens. Golf equipment manufacturers contributed to this trend by designing implements and balls that helped golfers get the ball into the air. There is sentiment among golfers and designers alike to bring the running shot back into the game and to realize that firmer turf, even if less green, is not always a sign of neglect.

The short twelfth at the Wild Dunes Links Course has a wild look and is fun to play. The fairway seems to tumble over natural dunes on this beautiful barrier island off the coast of South Carolina, although much of the hole was deliberately shaped for golf.

I think it's very likely that the growth patterns of golf and golf course design will continue to follow the economic times. It's been that way for a hundred years, and I can see no reason for that to change. Construction techniques are better, our knowledge is better, and the quality of the finished product is infinitely better. The National Golf Foundation, the organization that keeps track of these things, estimates that several hundred new golf courses per year will be built over the next

The tenth hole at Hudson National in New York plays from elevated tees to a fairway that bends to the right around a series of bunkers toward the Hudson River. Although modern construction techniques were used to build it, Hudson National has a very traditional look and feel.

decade. If so, I'd guess the growth will come in two areas: municipal and public courses, and in America's mid-size cities like Wilmington, Greensboro, Seattle, and other places where the population is growing and the baby-boom generation is nearing retirement.

One indicator of the growing interest in quality public golf facilities is a trend toward upscale public courses. Recognizing a market need in several places, owners have built golf complexes that rival the quality provided by most private clubs. We ourselves have designed half a dozen of these since 1990, including Emerald Dunes in West Palm Beach, Florida; Pelican Hill in Newport Beach, California; Hartefeld National in Avondale, Pennsylvania; Grayhawk in Scottsdale, Arizona; White Columns in Atlanta; and Pinehurst # 8 in Pinehurst, North Carolina, which, though owned by the resort, is operated from its own clubhouse and was designed in a private club mold.

The eighteenth green at Reynolds National in central Georgia (above) was formed into a tiny cape with water on the right, leaving room on the left for safe approach shots. The fairway bunker in the foreground provides strength to the left side of this medium-length par four and tends to bring the lake into the play. The tee at the eleventh hole at Emerald Dunes in Florida (opposite) is angled to the fairway so golfers can choose the amount of risk they want on this long par five. The aquatic plants along the water's edge and clusters of palms and dune grasses follow the themes of this course.

Playability

DESIGN PREFERENCES

One of the interesting things I've learned while writing this book is that words sometimes appear harsher when you see them in print. That isn't my normal style, and I've had to bend my natural inclinations occasionally in the interests of editorial clarity. So if you'll make allowances for the candor, I'll try to explain why I put little store in theories about golf design, and why they don't guide my own work.

Good friends and casual acquaintances alike have asked me to describe the philosophy I follow and, frankly, all the theories and philosophies seem to me nothing more than pleasant, but idle conversation. The truth is, I don't really have a philosophy. Granted, we need to follow certain principles and know what our priorities are when designing a golf course, but I don't believe we can allow them to dictate what fits on the site most naturally. I've always believed that the best approach to designing golf courses is to take the conditions and the priorities and fit them to the site. To do otherwise would be fighting the land.

Most of us understand that nature can make golf course designers look good.

The seventeenth at Iron Horse in Whitefish, Montana is a short par four that plays downhill through a narrow chute of lodgepole pines to a fairway that slopes left-to-right, with Whitefish Lake in the distance.

113

However, the standard cliché, that "mother nature can do it better" is true only up to a point. I don't believe nature can make great golf all by itself. In hilly or steep terrain like that found at Wade Hampton or Champion Hills in the mountains of western North Carolina, I think it's pretty obvious that you need to shape the land forms to create a quality golf setting and to produce acceptable shot values. That's where a golf course designer really earns his keep.

When I design a course, I think more in terms of design preferences. On any given site there are so many possible solutions, so many different ways of "carving the turkey" that I truly believe it's more difficult to follow a set philosphy than to allow the setting and the circumstances to suggest the design. That may sound simple, at first, and even a very obvious approach to designing golf holes, but it's the one that works best for me. A designer can't ignore his or her own preferences, and, in my opinion, he or she shouldn't. Each hole, as it proceeds, will require decisions about length, shape, bunker placement, green setting and shape, other hazards, contours, and so on, and all are subject to personal choice.

Here's an example: If I come to a hillside setting, my preference would be to design a hole with the high elevation on the right and the low one on the left, rather

The greenside bunker at the opening hole, a medium length par four, establishes a key design element at Bonita Bay East in Florida. The slopes, contours, and noses are characteristic of certain older, traditional golf courses and are treatments that answer a design goal for this course.

than the reverse. The reason is that a majority of golfers play golf with a left to right shape to their shots, a nice way of saying they slice the ball, and obviously they would have a tougher time playing a hole where the hillside is higher on the left because balls landing on the slope will bounce even farther to the right than normal. A major-

An aerial photo of the par four seventh at the Cotton Dike course on Dataw Island, South Carolina offers a perspective on how golf is designed to fit into natural surroundings. The lake in the center serves as both a water storage area and an open space amenity for several holes along the marsh.

115

ity of golfers are better off playing into a slope that is high on the right, which tends to deflect their shots back toward the center of the fairway. That would be my preference because I believe in designing golf courses that are playable by the greatest number of golfers, but it's certainly not a rule that all designers should follow. Once in a while, I might even design an exception on one of my own golf courses.

WHAT RULES?

We don't write down all the rules and principles, nor even concepts or lists of preferences. In fact, if someone asked me to write a manual of rules for golf course design, I would have to decline because, in my opinion, there are no rules. Compared to any rules or definitions we might list on a sheet of paper, I'm reasonably confident that the exceptions to those "rules" would fill up several volumes. That has been my experience, anyway. Those exceptions are what we look for because they make a golf course or an individual hole unique. As I said, I don't believe there is an ideal way to design a hole. It always gets down to personal preferences and who makes the final decision.

We have grown accustomed to the settings of American golf and, specifically, to the familiar shapes of certain holes at America's most famous golf courses, especially those that are seen frequently on television, but just because each of these holes was designed in a certain way doesn't mean that that's the only way, or even the right way. Cypress Point, Pine Valley, Oakmont, Winged Foot, all were fresh,

---

A fortress green was built at the par three seventeenth at the Golf Club of Oklahoma in Broken Arrow (top right) because of its location above a lake designed to handle flood surges of up to seventeen feet. The bunkers are staged so that, as water rises, they will always be visible and playable. (Bottom right) The flattish, irregular look of links golf is recreated at the eighth hole and others at Bayville Golf Club in Virginia Beach due to its setting near the sea. If we followed "rules," these greens might look different than they do, but not be as appropriate to the sites.

---

new designs when they opened, and some of them were quite different, perhaps even unusual for the time. Are the rolling, severely sloped greens at Augusta National, for example, the right way? They're neither right nor wrong, in my opinion, because there are no rules for these things. Every new golf course is a new experience, or should be, and the golf designer must be ready to impose his or her own vision and rules.

The East Course at Merion in Philadelphia is considered by many experts to be one of America's classic golf courses. The second and fourth holes are par fives, and those are the only par fives on the course. The par fives appear early in the routing because Hugh Wilson, the designer, thought they best fit the land that way. No rules, just his judgment. Cypress Point, another classic, has two par fives in a row in the middle of the course, then consecutive par threes toward the end. Alister Mackenzie was certain that the dictates of the land should override any "rules." Consider that Pine Valley, America's top ranked golf course in every

MIKE KLEMME/GOLFOTO

poll, is a par 70 golf course, yet many think of "championship" courses being at least par 71, if not par 72. What's more, Pine Valley's entry road crosses the eighteenth

fairway. When we start looking at all the exceptions, it's pretty clear that there are no hard and fast rules in this business.

In my own work, I prefer to avoid imitating past design work. In general, it's not a good policy to bring an idea from the last job, or one from a previous year, or even from something you read in Alister Mackenzie's book to a new project. If we did that, we'd probably fall short of our goal to make each golf course better than the last because the ideas would be stale. Or, we might be tempted to make something happen on a site that shouldn't be happening there, and that could be even worse. As golf designers, we do need to have as much knowledge as possible and allow that knowledge to inform our work as long as we keep our eyes open and look for the distinct differences on every piece of property, the details that can make a golf course

---

The fourth at Johns Island West in Florida (above left) is a par five that plays between trees and sand to a high green set into a prominent dune, one of several sand ridges that make this site unusual for Florida. The third on the West Course at Belfair in South Carolina (above right) is framed by a sprawling bunker and native "Angel" Oaks to the right and left of the green. Easier tees are provided to the right requiring less carry over the sand.

unique among its kind. Nothing is more valuable to our work, nor more appreciated by a client.

Our desire to avoid repetition of design doesn't mean we ignore a sound design solution. For example, we designed Johns Island West in Vero Beach, Florida in the 1990s on wonderful terrain that was blessed with tall sand ridges rising up to fifty feet high. The site was very much like the one we found at Jupiter Hills in the late 1960s. These two Florida courses are very different in design, yet we used a common design principle in both by placing greens and tees on the hillsides of some of the holes while routing the fairways into the flatter areas of the property.

This is a technique Donald Ross used in 1930 at Seminole, a golf course I consider one of the best routings of its time and one that continues to set a standard for

---

The first hole, a par four, establishes the environment golfers will encounter on the River Course at Kiawah Island Club (above left) with sweeping views of water, sand, native vegetation, and a stubborn, wind-swept pine. The par four twelfth at the Canyons at Bighorn (above right) has bunkers with long fingers designed to draw visual interest from the imposing mountain backdrop down to earth and into the foreground.

COURTESY OF WADE HAMPTON

how golf courses are designed. At Seminole, Ross found two sand ridges along the ocean separated by flat, sandy scrub and placed ten greens and eight tees on the ridges, with fairways stretching along the flats between them. We learned that lesson ourselves almost forty years later at Jupiter Hills, and there was every reason to follow such a sound design idea twenty years after that at Johns Island West. The differences in these courses lie in the details and in how those details are expressed.

THE DESIGN PROCESS

Generally speaking, I don't "see" a golf course in its final form when I'm designing it. That might surprise some people, but in the real world a golf course evolves

through each of its phases, which include design, earth moving, shaping, planting, landscaping, and tweaking. As I've mentioned, a golf course is not a static thing; it's an organic, growing thing. As designers and builders, we create a golf course as it's being built, as we mold it into the land. We constantly massage the details, and occasionally find more as we go along.

Of course, we need to have a quality design program which identifies the broad scope of a project. We want to know whether there will be forty-five bunkers or eighty, for example, and to calculate the approximate volume of earth to move so that a project can stay in line with a budget. We must also understand what is needed in the way of permits and environmental approvals because those will affect the duration and schedule of the project, as well as the budget. On the other hand, designing a golf course is quite different from designing a building where plans and drawings are required to be quite specific and exact. It might make some clients nervous knowing that the final product we deliver won't be exactly like the golf course shown on the plans and detailed diagrams, but a golf course cannot be constructed from plans alone.

The long, par four sixteenth at Wade Hampton in Cashiers, North Carolina is shown looking back towards Chimney Top Rock from green to landing area where mist rises from the lake on a cool, fall morning in the beautiful mountain setting of Western North Carolina.

The design process can be roughly outlined as follows: it usually starts with a telephone call from a client who wants to build a golf course. We begin by asking questions: What are the client's objectives, the concept, the timing, the schedule,

---

The approach to the final green at Edgewood Tahoe in Nevada (above) holds out risk and reward across water to a slender green in front of the handsome wood and glass clubhouse. This was one of our first high-end public courses. The eighteenth at The National in Toronto, Canada (opposite) plays across a pond to an angled fairway guarded by gaping bunkers and then rises to a plateau and the green beyond. The entire hole is visible from the elevated tee, announcing the challenges of this difficult finishing hole.

the market, and the resources? It is also important to discover a client's commitment to quality. These are usually general questions but necessary ones to see if we are comfortable with the project and can do what the client wants. I've had people call and say: "Come visit us tomorrow, and bring a contract. We'll give you a check, and you can start immediately." However, we do a limited number of golf courses each year, and our staff and resources are almost always committed in advance. We're not willing to drop or postpone a current

job for a new one because the most important golf course to us is the one we're presently working on, and the results of that work will determine our future.

The next step is to review topographic maps and other information about the site, and then visit the property. We've all heard stories about golf designers falling in love with a piece of land, and that still happens. But it's not the most important consideration any more, at least not to me, particularly in light of the advances in modern technology. The most important factor is the quality of the golf program the client wants to accomplish.

Finally, we try to evaluate the working relationship with each client. In the end, it's a people business, and we realize we'll be in partnership with the client in developing the overall program for golf. When determining where on the land the golf course will be located, for example, many factors must be taken into consideration, whether technical, financial, or environmental. As we work out the solutions to these and other questions, it's important for the chemistry and personalities of the people involved to blend smoothly.

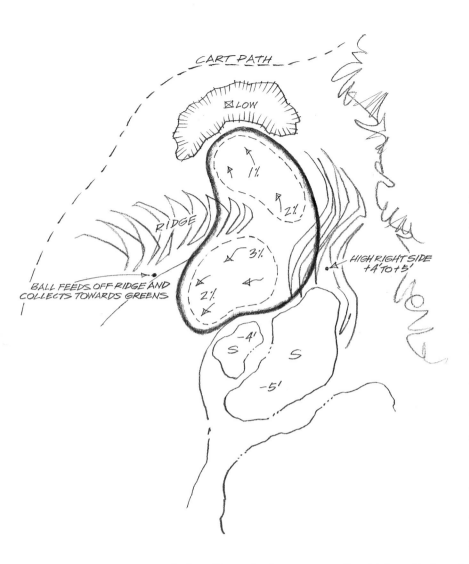

CART PATH

☒ LOW

RIDGE

BALL FEEDS OFF RIDGE AND
COLLECTS TOWARDS GREENS

HIGH RIGHT SIDE
+4' TO +5'

1%

2%

3%

2%

S -4'

S

-5'

Once we've gone through these introductions, we begin putting golf holes on paper. We may do five or six plans, each with different clubhouse locations requiring different starting and finishing points. This process not only gives the client a choice of where the course will start, it also helps us analyze the property to decide what is the best potential golf course for the site. Each project and site has its own priorities.

We prefer not to predetermine what par should be for any course we design, or what the ideal par should be for starting and finishing holes. Once designers get a fixed idea of what the length and par of the holes should be at the start or finish of the course, I wonder if all golf courses wouldn't start looking or playing alike. There's nothing wrong with holding to a design ideal, but I'd prefer to approach each site with an open mind and treat each one as a clean slate.

After we settle on how the golf course will fit on the site, we develop a grading plan. At this point, we are beginning to devise the eventual shape of the course and to see how the holes will flow through the property, while dealing with issues like site drainage and environmental impact. Drainage is of major importance because it relates to both the condition and appearance of the golf course, and most people judge the quality of a golf course by the way it looks.

Comprehensive drainage plans were not part of the original design programs on many of the older courses; they were added later. By contrast, golf course developers today budget up to $500,000 for proper storm drainage lines. One of the reasons is that golf courses are commonly placed on lower elevations of a property so that residual land uses can enjoy views overlooking the course. This means that water from the surrounding development drains onto the course, creating the need for a sound storm drainage system that will remove it in a sensible and lawful way.

Then we begin staking the golf course in the field and getting into some of the design details of each hole. Usually we place markings every hundred

feet so that we can see exactly where things fit and how the contours of the terrain work with our initial design concepts. Quite often, the base maps do not show detailed features of the property so we walk the site, checking these details. We also check the long range views and settings as we go, then go back and adjust the routing to take advantage of any interesting features like an unusual tree or rock outcropping. This process also gives us a realistic feel for the land and how it relates to golf. We may do a number of preliminary routing plans before settling on a final one.

An elevation sketch is prepared for each green setting showing percentages of elevation changes on and around the green. These are typically line drawings, as shown opposite, and are adjusted in the field as construction proceeds and the design is refined. These sketches also serve to indicate drainage patterns and placement of hazards. The seventeenth at Pinehurst # 8 (above) is a reachable par five that plays gradually downhill to a green situated on the far side of a marsh. The long, sandy margins and characteristic clumps of wire grass are typical of the Pinehurst area.

By this time, we have determined the location of the corridors for golf, tees, greens, bunkers, water features, practice range, maintenance facility, clubhouse, bridges, and shelters. We produce contract drawings, beginning with erosion control because erosion must be controlled before starting work on any site. After moving earth, we install drainage. This is followed by construction of greens and tees, detailed shaping and contouring, then installation of the irrigation system. The final steps are finish shaping of the greens and bunkers, grassing, circulation (maintenance trails, walking paths, and cart trails), and landscaping.

For those readers interested in more detail, we reproduce in the Appendix charts of guidelines used during both the design process and the construction process. These charts outline the stages each golf course project goes through. An indication of the detail required is seen by looking at the heading, "Clearing" on the Construction Process chart. For this item, we will detail how many acres will be cleared, how much hand clearing is required and how much by machine, and how the detail of the clearing will be carried out. Included in this item is specimen tree protection, for which we provide detail on fencing and other measures to preserve roots as well as trunks of trees.

The design process never stops until the grass goes into the ground, and even then we may still want to do some refinements. The finish work, things like fine tuning the edge of a bunker or the height of a greenside contour, is always an important part of the process. The differences in golf design are chiefly found in the artistic touches, which are the features most people refer to when they talk about differing styles of golf architecture.

Because of the technology available today, we can tackle difficult engineering

---

The par four thirteenth at Sand Ridge in Chardon, Ohio (opposite) was refined in the field to play past a rock outcropping and a natural waterfall to the right of the tee. Although the second shot plays downhill, this is one of the most demanding holes at Sand Ridge.

problems and mold land more easily than our predecessors could. But the fact that we have better resources is not an excuse to manipulate the landscape at will, nor to create unnecessary features. I can find no justification for creating something new and different just to put a signature on it, especially if the site is already wonderful. Making that sort of change seldom produces a golf course that looks real or natural, so we try not to over-create. I don't think that sentiment is particularly new, and I'm pretty sure it is shared by most golf course designers.

PETER WONG

With a few notable exceptions, I keep returning to the idea that the best golf course for any given site is one that most naturally fits the land. We certainly want to take advantage of and use all the latest technology in dealing with issues like drainage, engineering, and erosion control, or in moving volumes of earth. But even with advanced equipment and technology, we would prefer to get our inspiration from nature's own settings. These are usually the most attractive and satisfying to golfers. Because of better technology, our decisions are made easier and the work usually goes faster, but with the goal of embellishing nature, not obliterating it.

That's the way it should be. I grew up with the notion that golf architects who rely on the forms and materials of nature can't go far wrong. At the same time, in a profession like golf course design which is half art and half science, I think art must rule. Don't we see this in the golf courses we most admire? Unlimited resources should not, in my opinion, be used for their own sake just to manipulate the landscape, or to create an effect that is really not necessary. So often in our designs, it's what we leave out rather than what we put in that completes the picture most naturally and makes a hole fit our eye. The temptation to over-design is always there, and every so often we have to remind ourselves of this.

Much has been written about golf courses in the last twenty-five years that draws attention to novelty and innovation. Many books and essays have been published discussing the merits and details of the so-called classic golf courses versus the modern ones, while others describe every feature of the new golf courses as they

---

Shaping and placing greens that are well-protected yet fair is a constant goal. (Top left) This one awaits the end of the journey on the par five fifteenth at Reynolds National in north-central Georgia. The fairway comes in at the right where golfers can approach over land. (Bottom left) The green on the par five thirteenth at Spring Hill in Minneapolis is perched on a gentle slope at the end of a natural hillside with a strong bunker guarding the front right. The colors and contrasts of the wetlands on the right form an attractive frame, not to mention an imposing hazard, although an opening to the green is provided on the left side.

appear. Regardless of the itch to put a new face on things, to put a new twist on a story, there is very little, in my opinion, that's new in golf design; it has almost all been done and said before. Even the phrases used to describe golf courses have become cliches, or so it seems to me, and we can hope that we won't allow the work itself to become another. That's why we prefer not to write down a set way of doing things, but instead force ourselves to look at things with fresh eyes and to see each piece of property for its own possibilities..

PLAYABILITY

The classic tension in golf course design, as I see it, is not between risk and reward, but between playability and difficulty. Each day, every hour, we make decisions that affect how hard a golf hole will play. In my opinion, golf should not be easy, nor should it be overly difficult. We try to hit a middle ground between hard and easy so that, depending on how the course is set up, it can be made to play either fairly

DAVID S. SOLIDAY

hard or fairly easy. I believe golf courses should be designed along that middle ground because it is the one most likely to bring the greatest enjoyment to the greatest number of people. That's an old idea in golf, and one of the best.

Even if a client wanted to build the toughest course around, I would argue that it should be fair. In the days when I was working with my uncle, George Fazio, we designed one or two difficult golf courses at the insistence of the client. Butler National in Oak Brook, Illinois, comes to mind, a golf course that was built to be the permanent site of the Western Open and one that the pros voted the most difficult they had played up to that time. In addition, Butler National is a private men's club whose members wanted a big, challenging course, and they got it. While certainly tough by anyone's standards, I think Butler National is also fair for the type of clientele it was meant to serve, an opinion not shared by everyone who has played it, but one that became more and more apparent as the course matured.

A similar concept was adopted at The National in Toronto, Canada, built in that same era. The National is one of the strongest my uncle and I had designed up to that time, but even as we followed the client's call for challenge and difficulty, we

The eighteenth at Wild Dunes (opposite) is one of America's genuine links holes, giving the Links Course its name. This par five plays along sandy terrain flecked with wild grasses and sea oats on a curve of beach beside the Atlantic Ocean on the coast of South Carolina. The par five fifth at Barton Creek's Fazio Canyons (above) bends left following the natural slope of the land. The green is open in front allowing golfers to play approach shots along the ground and to allow the contour of the land to bring balls toward the hole.

paid a lot of attention to fairness and playability. This was a year or two after we had opened Butler National, and this golf club shared many of Butler's themes. It was a men's club and, like Butler National, there was a plan to bring a major tournament to The National. In fact, the Canadian PGA Championship was held there in 1979 when Lee Trevino beat Lanny Wadkins on the last hole to win the title. The founder, Gil Blechman, described the course this way: "The National builds up like a crescendo. It starts nice and quietly, then rolls through undulating land and keeps building until you come to the last two holes, where you have to hold your ears. You never saw two finishing holes like that in your life. The seventeenth was the favorite hole of the great Canadian player, George Knudson, where typically he had to hit a long, well-positioned drive followed by a middle iron into a small, elevated green with bunkers all around."

At the eighteenth hole, golfers must drive over part of a lake that continues down

---

The tees of the ninth hole at Dancing Rabbit's Azaleas Course in Mississippi (above) are set into dense forest. A creek crosses in front of the tees and follows the hole along the left side, winding around behind the elevated green. (Opposite) A picturesque green setting was found for the ninth hole at Maroon Creek in Colorado beneath the slopes of Aspen Highlands ski area which rises 5,000 feet above the putting surface. A deep-faced bunker nudges into the left side of the green.

the right side of the fairway. From there, all they can see is the top of the flag fluttering over the edge of the elevated green. It's a short par five, but full of risk and intimidation. In the Canadian PGA, when the eighteenth played as a par four, Trevino birdied the last four holes to win; nobody had done that before, and no one has since. The point is that The National is a terrific tournament course and the design concept met the client's objectives.

Normally in our discussions with clients, we rarely talk about the level of difficulty as a design goal. People in golf have come to understand that my design associates and I place a high value on the idea of "playability." This means that we try to design golf courses that are playable for all golfers, regardless of handicap. That probably sounds commonplace and obvious, but it's a goal we set for ourselves every single day. The tension comes in when we try to design a course that Davis Love and Fred Couples like to play — and we certainly think it's important that our golf courses have that reputation — with one that the average golfer will like and enjoy. Today, if a client asked me to build the hardest golf course in the region, I would try to talk him out of it, and if I couldn't, I would probably pass on the project.

In 1997, we designed Victoria National in an abandoned strip mine near Evansville, Indiana. Trenches fifty to seventy feet deep had been dug, and tailings from the mine operation had been piled on the site leaving berms and mounds along with pits and deep ravines, the sort of terrain one would never expect to find in southern Indiana. Every hole had potentially a dramatic setting, and it would have been easy to make each one a "finishing hole." The hard thing was to make sure we didn't.

The design preference at the par four seventeenth at Hartefeld National (above) in the historic countryside of eastern Pennsylvania was to place the green adjacent to the fence line that borders a road used by British troops during the Revolutionary War. (Opposite) The tenth green at Ventana Canyon in Tucson, Arizona was placed at the base of this unusual natural rock outcropping, referred to by locals as "The Whaleback." The preference here was to shape the greenside bunkers like "baby whales" on this short par four.

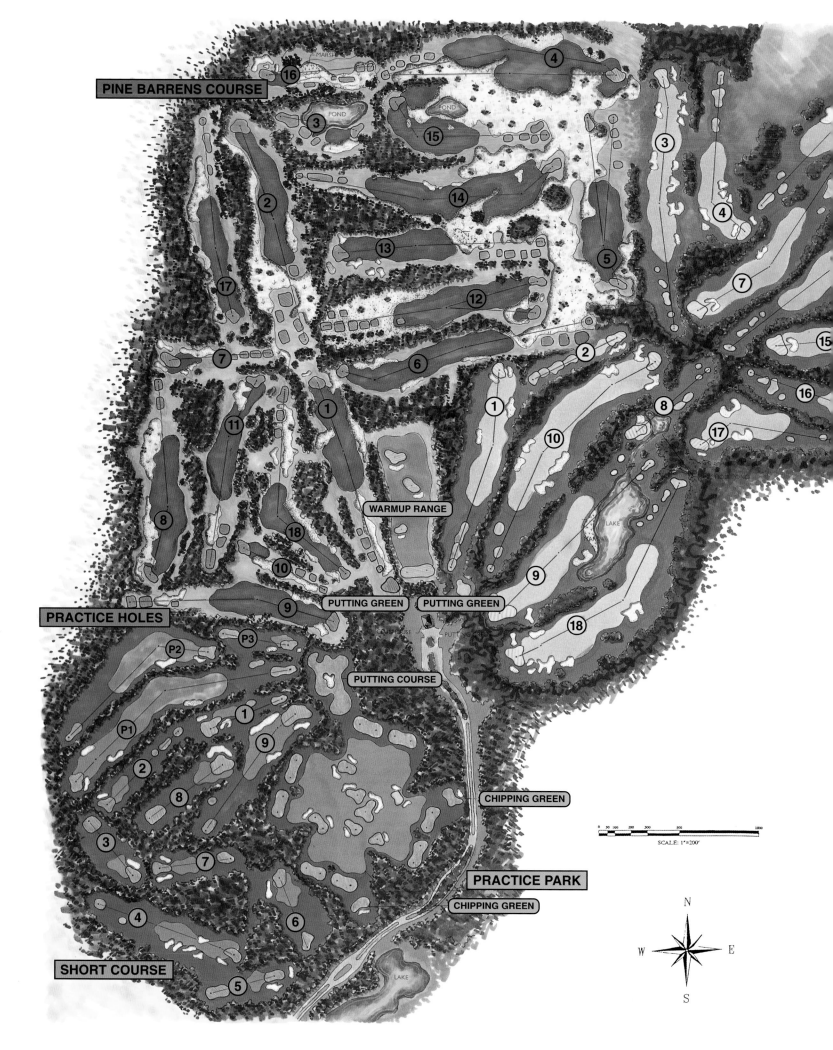

ROLLING OAKS COURSE

WORLD WOODS GOLF CLUB
A Cornucopia of Design Preferences

This graphic shows the full extent of the golf facilities at World Woods in Brooksville, Florida — two nationally-ranked courses featuring completely different design themes, a nine-hole short practice course, a 22-acre Practice Park that covers 360 degrees of the compass, three more individual practice holes (a par three, a par four, and a par five) and additional practice putting and chipping greens, bunkers for sand practice, and warmup ranges. Everything a golfer dreams of having is right there, open to the public, a project that was a golf architect's dream.

Rolling Oaks

HOLE	BACK TEES	PAR
1	395	4
2	172	3
3	519	5
4	341	4
5	458	5
6	322	4
7	409	4
8	148	3
9	437	4
OUT	3201	36
10	547	5
11	394	4
12	356	4
13	186	3
14	370	4
15	434	4
16	209	3
17	333	4
18	490	5
IN	3319	36
TOTAL	6520	72

FORWARD TEES
5245
TOURNAMENT TEES
6985

Pine Barrens

HOLE	BACK TEES	PAR
1	371	4
2	428	4
3	146	3
4	480	5
5	362	4
6	518	5
7	185	3
8	361	4
9	395	4
OUT	3246	36
10	158	3
11	379	4
12	457	4
13	421	4
14	527	5
15	313	4
16	205	3
17	376	4
18	376	4
IN	3212	35
TOTAL	6458	71

FORWARD TEES
5301
TOURNAMENT TEES
6902

Short Course

HOLE	BACK TEES	PAR
1	205	3
2	207	3
3	150	3
4	308	4
5	148	3
6	198	3
7	158	3
8	182	3
9	286	4
TOTAL	1842	29

MIDDLE TEES
1596
FORWARD TEES
1339

Practice Holes

HOLE	BACK TEES	PAR
1	513	5
2	361	4
3	128	3

We had to remind ourselves to stick with the basics as we designed each hole. Is it playable? Will people enjoy playing it? Will the mid-level golfer have fun? Will he or she feel challenged, yet not overly penalized? How will the high handicapper play it? How will the forward tee players fare? And, equally important, how does the person playing from the back tees respond? On a site like Victoria National, you're often tempted to make the holes a bit too difficult for the good player. The danger lies in making it too difficult, or even extreme.

In hilly or mountain terrain, it is easier to design a wide variety of golf holes because of the long views and often dramatic settings provided by the natural elevations. You can easily exhaust your adjectives, from awesome to sensational, in places like Maroon Creek in the mountain valleys of Colorado, or at Wade Hampton in the mountains of western North Carolina. The views are spectacular, yes, but the downside is that golf does not readily fit into hilly or mountainous terrain. As designers, we must decide where and how to adjust the terrain for golf. Usually, a golf course designer fights the uneven landscape in an attempt to create platforms for golf while trying to preserve the natural appearance of the site. The real task in that circumstance is to blend golf with severe terrain and emerge with a balance between the two that golfers will hardly notice.

It is a truism of American golf that the better players tend to play golf in the air, and the poorer players tend to play golf along the ground. As designers, we must be

---

*The long sixteenth at Champion Hills in North Carolina (top right) takes advantage of intersecting creeks,
playing across one and following another that flanks the right side of the hole all the way to the green.
The eighteenth at Old Overton in Alabama (middle) runs along the base of a "high wall" created by mining
operations to a green where undulations tie-in and balance the high relief on the right. The par four fourteenth
at Pablo Creek in Jacksonville (bottom) has a natural look to it because very little was done
to embellish it. The hole follows the edge of Pablo Creek and a marsh, bending to
an open green set among tall, mature oaks.*

---

mindful of this. At the same time, if we want to create the best settings for golf and the best golf holes, we need to provide for both styles of play. It is perfectly all right to design holes that require good golfers to play through the air, so long as the high handicap golfers are not forced to follow them, because, if that were to happen, the less gifted golfers might be eliminated from the game.

We know that expert players, the Greg Normans and David Duvals, have highly developed skills and can control the ball better and more consistently than, say, a good amateur who is perhaps the club champion. We know, too, that as a golfer's handicap approaches double-digits, he or she has even less control of golf shots. At some level as their handicaps rise, golfers have less and less idea of where the ball is going. Even when they hit a good shot, they are uncertain how or why it happened. This golfer probably hits a fair percentage of shots along the ground, and fewer than he or she might wish through the air.

In our view, higher handicap golfers deserve a fair chance at the green, although it might cost them more

strokes. So when we design hazards with these golfers in mind, we put the hazards in a more or less direct path for the target so that expert golfers who can fly the hazard will earn an advantage for his or her skill. The less skilled golfer who prefers not to risk the hazard must play on an angle away from the hole to stay safe, but he or she will certainly need to take more strokes. This is common design practice because it keeps faith with the basic idea that skill should be rewarded, if luck doesn't find you first.

Examples are everywhere, and they can be obvious or even subtle, at times. The first hole at Pelican Hill in Newport Beach, California, plays down the hill with a tremendous view of the ocean. The huge scale and beauty of the property, the visual strength of the setting tends to overcome golfers, at first, and this distraction in it-self is a subtle kind of hazard. The green is angled leftward from the right side of the fairway, so the hole opens from the right side where most golfers tend to play.

In addition, the fairway slopes from right to left so slicers can drive with some confidence that their errant tee shots will bounce back toward the fairway. If they miss the second shot on the right, they still have plenty of room and a good angle from which to chip or pitch onto the green.

Providing multiple tees that allow a hole to be played at different lengths is basic to accommodating different classes of golfers, and has been a standard in the industry for many years. In my mind, however, yardage alone is not the most important consideration in achieving playability. We could build a relatively short golf course

---

A grand view of Lake Tahoe is captured at the fourteenth tee (opposite) at Edgewood Tahoe in Nevada. The eighteenth on the Hills Course at Jupiter Hills in Florida (above) plays from the top of one high dune ridge to another and calls for a long, difficult second up the slope to the hilltop green framed by pines and Florida skies. "Playable" doesn't mean "easy"; holes like these reward skill yet are fair to the average golfer.

of, say, 5,400 yards, but if we placed perpendicular hazards every 150 to 200 yards, someone would be bound to shoot a high score and a poor player simply couldn't play it. This leads us to design open target areas from tee to green that allow golfers who aren't experts to play away from bunkers and other hazards and still have an opening to the greens.

The placement of hazards is critical to making the game more enjoyable for large numbers of golfers. We know that perpendicular hazards — bunkers, streams, or rough areas that cross the fairway — make the game more difficult for higher handicap golfers than for good players. What we call target golf — playing through the air to particular target spots — makes for very difficult golf courses because the ball must carry rough areas or hazards to reach safe ground.

Sometimes we can't avoid designing a few holes of target golf. Typically in the

desert areas, state and environmental regulations limit how much grass is allowed. As a result, golf designers are compelled to create a version of target golf where golfers play from one island of turf to another. Generally speaking, target golf of this kind means playing golf through the air, and, in many cases, golfers are forced to carry the ball from tee to fairway. At Estancia in Scottsdale, Arizona, we had some of those conditions on a property filled with large boulders. It is a spectacular site, so we were motivated to preserve the great natural setting while reducing to a minimum the need to play from island to island of turf. Fortunately, there were only a few places where the rocks and natural environment dictated carries over rough terrain. There's a steep ravine at one hole, the eleventh, a neat little par three that plays through a peek-a-

boo cleft in the rocks. In most other places, we were able to bring the edges of the fairways closer to the tee boxes in an effort to keep long carries from the tees to a bare minimum.

Playability, as I define it, is lowered on these "target style" courses, and cer-

The traditional shapes and understated features of Forest Creek (above) are typified by the par four sixteenth, winding over sand hills and through the pine forests of Pinehurst, North Carolina, an ideal setting for golf. The opening hole at Johns Island West in Florida (opposite) offers a gentle welcome to a strong course with just a touch of strategy required to negotiate the tall pine on the right and the single bunker on the left side of the green.

tainly this is true for higher handicap golfers. Yet a course that is playable, in my terms, does not have to be easy. Pinehurst # 2, where the 1999 U. S. Open was held, is not an easy course by anyone's standards yet has almost no perpendicular hazards and can be played along the ground from beginning to end. It has some of the most challenging green complexes in golf, but is very playable, very strong, and very fair. The placement and the size of hazards have much more to do with the playability of a hole than how many there are. The fact that a golf course had fifty or a hundred

---

The sixteenth hole on Pelican Hill's Ocean Course South in Newport Beach, California plays into prevailing ocean breezes over a ravine to a green that is tied into the natural ridge on the left. The ocean appears to be fairly close to the green, but it's actually about 700 yards away.

144

sand bunkers wouldn't necessarily indicate how hard or easy it is. But knowing *where* the bunkers are located in relation to the line of play, and how large they are, would give me a clue. For example, if a bunker is located back and left of a green, it would not create the same difficulty as a bunker cut into the front right of the same green. Also, a large bunker is generally more of a problem than a small one and, in simple terms, the farther from the edge of the green, the harder the shot. Long bunker shots are probably the hardest shots in golf, even for the great players. We are always par-

---

Attempting to carry the bunker on the far side of the lake is for brave souls at the fourteenth, a long par four at Victoria National in southern Indiana. The lakes were created by open-pit mining, the ridges by spoils from the excavations; the vegetation grew up over the years.

The theme and texture of native fescue grasses surrounding the tees on the second hole at Hallbrook in Leawood,
Kansas is repeated as a frame on a hillside behind the green. The target is open on the right to give weaker hitters
a fair chance, while the left side is fortified by contours and a steep-faced bunker against those
who would try boldly for the flag.

ticular about the placement of hazards, but even more so on long holes where the average golfer is likely to take the most strokes.

It's true that golf course designers are tempted, at times, to design bunkers or other features for visual impact where they really are not necessary. This tends to happen when designers sense something is wrong with a hole, and usually it's because they've built too much into it, not too little. Sometimes it happens because the designer or the client is trying to make a statement. I suppose that's only human nature, but we're better off resisting those temptations.

In general, we consider these guidelines before designing a golf hole: (1) avoid long bunkers on the right sides of holes where high handicappers have a tendency to play the ball; (2) create openings to the green so golfers can reach the putting surface along the ground from at least one direction; (3) avoid a design that forces golfers to play entirely through the air; (4) provide more playing area in the fairway in places where the high handicap golfer tends to miss shots.

These are simple precautions, subject to exceptions when the terrain or circumstances dictate, but rarely taken without a pang of conscience and never without considering the interests of the vast majority of golfers.

The eighth hole at Thornblade in Greenville, South Carolina can be set up to play harder by placing the hole on the left side of the green, as shown above, or easier by moving the pin away from the bunkers and creek on the left to the more open right side of the green.

147

We are always concerned about how we treat the right side of the golf course because that's where the majority of golfers play the game. Statistically, there are more high than low handicappers in golf, and high handicappers tend to slice or push

———————————————

The fourteenth at the Pinehurst # 8 Centennial Course is shaped along the edge of an old marsh area. The tempo builds at this par four, leading as it does into the strong finishing holes, and is designed so that pin placements on the left side of the green will flirt with the marsh.

———————

the ball, which puts them on the right side of the golf course most of the time. However, we wouldn't place all the hazards on the left side of the hole just to keep the right side free for high handicappers. There ought to be a balance to this. Part of our

---

A rolling, undulating green nestles into the sand barrens at the end of the par five fourteenth on the Pine Barrens Course at World Woods in Florida. The contours and movement in and around the green induce an ever-changing and fascinating variety of shots to its many possible pin positions.

---

job is to recognize where in the terrain it might fit best to put bunkers or other hazards on the right, and to have the judgment to know how often to do it. Golf designers may differ on how to handle this, and I think that's perfectly acceptable; one version or opinion is as good as another. The final judgment will be rendered by the golfers themselves; will they like the golf course or not?

All or nothing holes have an honored place in the game because they add drama and excitement to a round of golf. I like playing them myself, it's just that I look for alternative routes when I design a hole. In general, I would prefer to see par three holes play downhill. Everyone loves to stand on an elevated tee and look down to the green site, and it seems to me that the par threes that tend to stay most in our memory play down to the green. My next preference would be for par threes where the tee and green are on the same level, but with a depression between them. That perspective tends to give the impression that the green is elevated even when the tee and green are at the same elevation. A good example is the third hole at Ventana Canyon in Tucson, a short par three that plays from the edge of one rock outcropping to another. (Incidentally, because of its exposure to temperature extremes in the southwestern desert, this green is equipped with both heating and cooling systems under the surface; at the time it was built, this was the only green in the United States to be so equipped.) Another is the thirteenth hole at Black Diamond near Florida's west coast, which plays across a huge abyss and is a dramatic entrance to its famous quarry holes. I would try to avoid building par threes that play uphill

Contours and bunker depths combine with water and wind to establish the character of Karsten Creek in Oklahoma (opposite). The eighteenth at Estancia in Scottsdale, Arizona (above), plays from a high tee over a patch of desert to a fairway that turns left past two nests of bunkers that tend to focus golfers' attention on the task and away from the rugged terrain surrounding them. The fairway is wider than it looks, and there is ample room short and right of the green.

151

The finishing hole at Stock Farm in Hamilton, Montana (above) winds through the wilderness past mature ever-greens with the snowy peaks of the Bitterroot Mountains in the distance. The bunkers announce themselves from the elevated tee, offering helpful signposts for golfers' strategies on this long par four. When working in wide open spaces, the edges of a hole are often a distinctive design feature. At Primm Valley in the Nevada desert (top right) shadows creep across the tenth fairway and bring the contours, bunkers, and native grasses alongside the fairway into bold relief. Rocks are used on the eighteenth at the Canyons at Bighorn in California (bottom right) to indicate vertical separations and provide framing, a treatment inspired by the rocky, desert environment.

because golfers like to see where the ball lands on short holes.

In this book, we showcase more than fifty golf courses which contain a total of about one thousand separate golf holes, and we'll be opening another five or six golf courses — yet another hundred holes — during the year following publication of this book. I think I'm correct in saying that none of these holes look like any of the others. That's nothing special; the reason can be found in those exceptions to the rule we mentioned earlier, and the fact that we look for the exceptions all the time.

I've heard it said that all the land suitable for golf courses has been taken. In my opinion, that's not remotely close to the truth. Within the past decade, we've been given previously unworkable sites in dramatic settings, courses like Pelican Hill along the steep coastal slopes of California and Hudson National along the banks of the Hudson River in New York, or in previously unimaginable settings like Primm Valley and Shadow Creek

in the barren Nevada desert. Off hand, I'd guess there are about a million excellent potential golf course sites in the continental United States today. Even if it's only half that number, my point is that there are more sites than we'll ever use and no reasons why anyone can't or shouldn't build a great golf course on any one of them. It would be largely a matter of commitment and of how hard someone is willing to work at it. The future of golf course design looks very healthy to me.

ELEMENTS OF DESIGN

Twenty years ago, I was asked by a client to draw up a list of the most important criteria to look for when choosing a site for a golf course. The client was John Williams, a member of Augusta National and Southern Hills in Tulsa. He and a group of friends had decided they wanted to build a world-class private course in Tulsa that would be "as good as anything in golf," and wanted the list to help them in scouting for an ideal site in and around Tulsa.

That was about the time we were designing The Vintage Club in Indian Wells, California, Wild Dunes in Charleston, South Carolina, and PGA National in Palm Beach Gardens, Florida, and the list I provided for Mr. Williams included seven elements I thought would help the Oklahoma men achieve their goal. They were: sandy loam soil (which is hard to find in Oklahoma), rolling terrain, reasonable tree cover, a lake or stream, good access, water recharge availability, and good drainage. Eventually, the Williams group found a suitable piece of property in Broken Arrow, near Tulsa, where we designed and built the Golf Club of Oklahoma. It

---

The eighth hole at Long Point Club on Amelia Island in Florida is laid along the gentle sand ridges of this barrier island and is ringed by massive live oaks.

had all but one of the items on my list, and turned out to be one of our finest designs.

Today, that list of essential elements would be a lot smaller. In fact, we've come to the conclusion that only one item on the list is indispensible for golf: Access to a

This view of the final fairway at Champion Hills in North Carolina looks back from the green past a creek that flanks it on the right (left of the picture) to tees stepped into the hillside and faced with solid walls of rocks collected from the creek.

sufficient water supply to irrigate the turf. Even if the land were without features, we could create them by moving enough earth. If the property were without tree cover, we could plant trees, even big ones. We can create just about anything today, but without water, you can't have golf.

Even Shadow Creek in Las Vegas, where we almost built the golf course out of thin air, had to have water; it was piped in from the municipal water supply at considerable expense. We shaped the course from flat desert

land, excavated huge canyons and depressions, built a large berm around the edge of the property, had mature trees trucked in, and created wonderful streams and aquatic features, but the water made everything work. The only other ingredient that might be desirable, though not essential, in choosing a site for a new course is the presence of natural relief and movement in the land. This would primarily affect financial requirements in that a client would not have to spend money creating interesting features in essentially dull terrain, or in dealing with, say, a bed of rock immediately under the soil where blasting might be required.

Today, we often use recycled water to irrigate golf courses. Runoff from a site is reprocessed, removing any impurities and toxins, and that water supplies the daily

---

The terrain at the par four fifth at Sand Ridge in Ohio offered two ideal green settings; since we didn't want to give up either one, we built both, separated by a massive bunker. This was an obvious opportunity to serve the cause of variety.

needs of turf and water features. Thirty years ago, we didn't know how to recycle water, and we certainly didn't think about why it might be necessary. Now, we don't have to worry about golf courses taking supplies of drinking water from wells and reservoirs. It's good for the environment, good for us, and the recyled water is good for the golf courses. Everybody wins.

Years ago, golf courses were not irrigated as much as they are today. The demand for lush turf was not as widespread, probably because most golf courses were built and operated along very practical lines. Many of us grew up playing on what we called "cow pastures." In Philadelphia, I played on municipal courses and didn't realize until I was about twelve that you were supposed to have grass on the tees. We teed off from rubber mats on some courses, or just plain dirt.

For years, members at exclusive clubs like Newport Golf Club in Rhode Island, one of the five founding clubs of the United States Golf Association, didn't bother to water the fairways because people in the early decades of American golf were more accustomed to playing on drier turf. The tees in those days were smaller, too, with an area of probably one or two thousand square feet on a par three hole where traffic is high. They were always worn out, even at the better public courses. For a public course today, we build tees on par three holes that measure up to nine thousand square feet in area.

In the past, only the greens, tees, and approaches to greens were watered. Today, people want quality, and they equate quality with lush turf, so in many cases they water the whole golf course — even the roughs! That alone has created a major change, not only in maintenance practices and sensitivity to the environment, but in the playability of golf courses and in how they are designed. On the positive side,

---

The twelfth at Belfair's West Course in the South Carolina Low Country (opposite) plays alongside an interior lake to a shallow, angled green beyond a spreading oak. To preserve the oak, small bunkers were placed in front of the green so the hole could be played as a short but testing par five.

this has helped create giant open spaces, particularly in metropolitan and suburban areas, huge green lungs in the midst of modern civilization's concrete and steel.

The first thing we consider when approaching the design of a new golf course project is its concept. Will it be a public, private, or resort golf course? Will the golf course stand alone, or will real estate be an important part of the development? Will the golf course be designed principally for the benefit of medium to high handicappers, or for single handicap players? Will the golf course occupy less desirable land —

The par three fifth hole on the Raptor Course at Grayhawk, a resort course in Scottsdale, Arizona plays across native desert to a green set along an existing grade on the left. A steep slope is carved into the ground on the right and a grassy area provided beneath it for shots that stray in that direction.

say, lowland or barren wasteland — or be given prime location — say, waterfront or lush, rolling meadowland? Where will the clubhouse and entry roads be located? Is the financing sound, and will the budget allow for high profile design treatments, or will there be limitations on what can be planned for the golf course?

It's also important for a designer to know whether resources are in place to provide for appropriate finish work like landscaping, concealed cart paths (which we favor), clubhouse arrangements, golf course and grounds maintenance, the screening of unsightly views, and other factors that will influence the level of quality and perceptions of the golf course. Other considerations that may influence the concept are the terrain and the style of golf the client wants.

VARIETY AND PRIMARY ELEMENTS

Once a concept has been decided, the elements we consider foremost as we undertake the design of a golf course are variety, playability, aesthetics, and challenge. Playability was discussed at some length in the previous chapter as an important part of the design preferences we favor, although it could just as well be considered among the primary elements of our golf designs. With that in mind, we can explore other design elements and the ways they influence our work, beginning with variety.

We always want to achieve variety in the design of golf holes and of the golf shots required, along with the visual impressions golfers have when standing on the tees. Our objective is to create golf courses where each hole has a distinctive look and character so that, hopefully, golfers will remember it after the round is over. When golfers walk off a course after the round and can't remember how they played a hole, it's usually because they can't remember the hole. If they can visualize a hole later where they may have played a memorable shot — whether good or bad — or that formed an indelible impression in their minds, it adds to the enjoyment of the experience. Our memories preserve our experiences, as golfers and as individuals, and as golf design-

The par four seventh at Spring Hill in Minnesota (above) plays across a marsh and angles uphill through the forest
to a rolling green. Forward tees are located at the far left of the picture where golfers are not required to play over the
hazard. (Top right) A brook crosses the par three thirteenth at Dancing Rabbit's Azaleas Course in Mississippi, but
the bunkers on the right side of the green are the principle obstacle. A glance should tell golfers that taking more club
and playing to the left is the wise choice. (Bottom right) The ninth hole at Flint Hills National in Wichita, Kansas is
a strong par four bending from right to left around a lake. The contours on the right are meant to help golfers who
choose to play safely to that side of the fairway, but the safe way may be the hard way when the flag is on the right.

ers we look for the settings that will frame those memories.

Nature doesn't do things by rote; it creates unique features and shapes out of rocks, trees, and hills. No two pieces of land are alike. We could break up all the available land in the continental United States into two hundred acre parcels, and each would be different from its neighbor, however slightly. The Almighty doesn't create six billion people exactly alike, as we know, and nature behaves the same way with property.

The possibilities of any given site are almost limitless, which is why golf course design can be so varied and interesting. Even when blessed with a wonderful site, however, a golf course would be quite boring if we built all the holes alike. Suppose, for example, we had a setting alongside the ocean. If each of the eighteen holes exhibited the same tendencies, what a dull course it would be. Or imagine a site in the mountains with a feature like the sheer face of Chimney Top

Rock at Wade Hampton. No matter how great or how dramatic each hole might be, if every one were laid out underneath that landmark, the golf course would become so monotonous golfers wouldn't remember many of the holes. Varying the design of holes feeds our natural curiosity and satisfies that itch of anticipation. Variety is more than the spice of life; it's the life of golf.

We all remember the story of Ben Hogan achieving such precision that he played from the same divots he left the day before, but if we all hit the same shots from the same spots day after day, week after week, we'd soon grow tired of golf. One of the great fascinations of the game is the many different kinds of shots we are required to play; another is how differently the holes appear to our eyes, the rich variety of the landscapes we're invited to explore. Nature is endlessly varied, and, in my opinion, so are the best of our golf courses.

ROUTING A COURSE

By seeking variety, I do not mean that we should try to mix the style of a golf course. Instead, I mean that we should try to vary the shapes of the holes and the green settings, and to vary the angles into the greens. If all the greens were down in valleys, or all were pushed up above the fairways, it wouldn't matter how fine the contours were or whether we surrounded the greens with wonderful trees or not because the green settings would look pretty much the same. We should look for variation in the elevations — uphill, downhill, and flat — and in the placement of hazards along the routes of play.

How many holes will be straight, how many will bend left to right, and how many right to left? How will the par fives vary in yardage and conformation so that some are genuine three-shotters while others will skirt hazards to offer a reward for risking a long or dangerous shot? How will the par threes be oriented as to the four directions, and how will these short holes compare with the longer ones in taking advantage of the prevailing winds and angles of sun? Equally important, what are the unique features of

The par three sixth on the The River Course at Kiawah Island Club in South Carolina plays across colorful muhly grass and a wide lake. A pond stocked with bass lies beyond the green. Variety is served by the unusual shaping of the hole and by contrasts in the colors and textures of the vegetation.

A wide, sprawling bunker on the par five fourteenth (above) is an example of a treatment at Johns Island West in Vero Beach, Florida where sand is an integral part of the environment and shadows creeping across the fairway add deception to the task of judging distances. (Opposite) To reach the wide green on the sixteenth hole at Karsten Creek in Oklahoma golfers must thread a shot between treeline and bunkers on this long par four.

the site that we want to embellish and preserve? All of these questions, and more, will be asked before we satisfy our own, and every golfer's, appetite for variety. Occasionally I'm asked what the ideal starting hole should be. What is the ideal length and par for an opening hole? What is the ideal finishing hole? Where should the first par three be? Such questions are fine for cocktail party conversations, but the truth is I don't think about "ideal" holes, nor do I try to follow a standard routing. What matters is what fits best on the land; that determines what and where the starting and finishing holes will be, and all the holes between. We can't begin every course with a par five that bends to the right, and wouldn't want to.

Sometimes, we choose the routing of a golf course for reasons you wouldn't guess. At Reynolds National in the wooded hills of central Georgia, the property has many steep ravines. One of the largest was very attractive but too wide for a golf hole, and the sides were too steep for real estate. Since it was not really suitable for golf or housing, the solution was to build a huge practice range there, an unusual and attractive setting for practicing golf.

This dictated where the start and finish of the golf course would be. That was the first time I had been involved in a project where the location of the practice range determined the layout of rest of the golf course. Once again, this fit our normal program of having no preconceived notions about a design other than to take the land as we found it and allow the terrain to suggest what should be done.

Every golf course, in a sense, is like a painting. Each one has grass, sand, some change in elevation (even if only slight), native vegetation, perhaps water, and usually trees. Some sites have marshes, creeks, and beautiful trees with overhanging branches. Those are the paints we use, and the golf course the painting. We use different brushes and brush strokes to create the effects we want, and change colors when appropriate. Just as in a fine painting, the ingredients — the paints — don't vary, but each painting is unique in the sense that it reflects that particular subject, or, in our case, a particular site. With those half dozen or so paints, we try to create eighteen different scenes and, taken all together, a finished canvas that comprises a golf course. We do that about six times a year, and the next year another six, and so on year after year. Each one has its own features and personality and is designed to its own image, and each one we hope, will be different and better than its predecessor.

AESTHETICS AND SECONDARY ELEMENTS

Part of the enjoyment of golf lies in the visual experience of wandering through a fine landscape and feasting our eyes on the natural scenery. For this reason, we pay attention to the placement of greens and especially tees that offer attractive, long-range views. As much as we can, we want to draw the beauty of the surrounding areas into the golf course by revealing it to golfers particularly in those spots where they

---

The par three seventeenth at Conway Farms in Lake Forest, Illinois is designed to capture the broad setting and open spaces of the site. Tees and green are framed by native grasses rippling in the breezes, a constant accompaniment to golf in this region. Thickets of dwarf pine and plum add to the pleasing contrasts in vegetation.

pause while driving or putting. Often we will find an attractive natural feature like a lake or stream that is not even part of the property, but with a little effort we can make it a visual focal point for the golf course.

We laid out the holes at Hudson National to expose the wonderful, long range views of the Hudson River that flows several hundred feet below the property. That was an obvious decision, although it did take some effort to shape golf holes across the tall bluffs because of the hard granite rock just under the surface. The effect is particularly striking at the par three sixteenth hole, which plays from a high tee toward the river and down to the green. A very different example is the way we used the distant mountains at Shadow Creek in Las Vegas as the primary visual backdrop in an otherwise flat, unattractive desert environment. We surrounded the golf course with a berm on which we planted vegetation to screen the desert floor while allowing long range views of the nearby Spring and Sunrise Mountains.

Sometimes we are adventurous in our pursuit of aesthetics. At Maroon Creek in Aspen, Colorado, we more or less suspended two par threes along the creek to capture the sense of excitement and grandeur of the site. The holes were placed on the edge of a cliff about fifty or sixty feet above Maroon Creek and provide stunning platforms for the awesome views across the tall ravine and back up the mountainside to the slopes of the Aspen Highland skiing area.

From the moment we walk the property and put stakes in the ground we're thinking about the aesthetic features and the small artistic touches we'd like to incorporate in the design. Most of the time we can't see these on a topographic map, but

---

The eleventh at the Golf Club of Tennessee (top right) moves through dense vegetation past a center bunker that offers multiple options of how to play the hole. An open savannah on the left was converted into marsh and revegetated, creating both a nature preserve area and a strong visual presence to balance the well-defined ridges on the right. (Bottom right) The rolled, scalloped edges and rocks on the approach to the par five fifth at Emerald Dunes in West Palm Beach are a little different from the usual Florida lakeshore.

we see them in the field. When we begin clearing the property, for example, we look for specimen trees to be saved — trees of a certain age and height or ones with a perfect shape, and others with a unique shape. It's always important to keep the understory as well, as it helps define the natural setting and may also harbor dogwood, holly, cedar, or other attractive species. If they happen to be in the way of a fairway, we transplant them.

At Champion Hills in North Carolina, we encountered an abundance of rocks that would have to be buried or sold. But it was a particularly attractive rock and we felt it shouldn't be disposed of, so we decided to use it as an accent in building tees, restraining walls for the cart paths, and waterfalls. The rocks provided an unusual texture that contrasted with the turf and thick mountain vegetation of rhododendron, oak, and mountain laurel. This was an aesthetic decision as much as a practical one.

A combination of aesthetic

and environmental factors might rule our design choices. Belfair is located in the South Carolina low country noted for its gorgeous specimen trees. The twelfth hole was designed as a lovely three-shotter around Hidden Lake to a big green resting underneath a marvelous old oak. The hole was on the short side, but we didn't want to lose the tree. We created three pot bunkers in front of the green and now golfers lay up short and hit a pitch of sixty to one hundred yards over the bunkers into a

shallow green. It's probably the hardest shot on the golf course, and a fascinating one.

In the early 1990s, we were asked to design a course near Nashville for a group that was forming the Golf Club of Tennessee. The site was almost too good. A gorgeous stream named Brushy Creek, a tributary of the Harpeth River that runs through Nashville and eventually empties into the Cumberland River, ran through the property, cutting through lovely hillside settings and flowing into a big valley. The natural terrain around that part of Nashville is filled with beautiful changes in elevation

---

The sixteenth on the Mountain Course at The Vintage Club in Indian Wells, California (opposite) with its brilliant flower accents rises gradually past a series of lakes and cascades to a shallow green sloped from back to front. Not long by modern standards, this 406-yard par four is among the toughest and most distracting in golf. The par five fifteenth at Barton Creek's Fazio Foothills Course (above) plays on a ridge above Barton Creek and finishes at an angled green cut into a high slope on the right, a feature designed to help golfers work the ball back towards the green.

and mature trees, rock outcroppings, and sheer cliff walls. Over the ages, the valleys were created by glaciers and erosion, leaving some of the most interesting settings for golf holes we've ever encountered.

We found literally hundreds of potential holes on that site and probably drew

---

Finding natural sites for tees and greens is one of the initial steps in routing studies. The ninth hole at Caves Valley in Owings Mills, Maryland occupies a beautiful setting in the country, traveling slightly uphill alongside a creek on the right to a green set into the woods, and some golfers think this is the strongest par four on the course.

three dozen different course routings. A year later, we returned to the site because I was anxious that perhaps we hadn't found the best locations. I told my staff to walk the property once again and make sure we had chosen the right locations. "Everyone has high expectations for the course, and we have a great opportunity here, but let's

------

The choice of tee and green settings is influenced both by technical and by aesthetic values. The sixth at Hartefeld National in Pennsylvania looks almost like a postcard with its green nestling between bunkers across a lake. It sits beneath a manicured lawn leading to the stately manor house that serves as clubhouse and fine restaurant at this former estate.

make sure we don't miss anything," I said. It was worth the effort. Brushy Creek touches about half the holes in one way or another, and the most dramatic terrain features fit the holes naturally.

We didn't get any smarter; we just worked a little longer. When a golf designer finds a spectacular site, it's natural to say wonderful things about what might be created there. But talk is cheap; the only thing that counts are results. What comes out in the end is not an accident, and it's not luck. What matters most are all the old cliches, like hard work, commitment, dedication, and finally just getting the job done. We can get lucky once, maybe twice, or even three times. But when we do five or six golf courses a year, as we do every year, the luck wears off quickly.

As many as a dozen site plans and two or three dozen routing plans may be drafted for a given project, each one with different options and possibilities. Some people refer to these drafts as designs, but I do not. A designer can draw all the pretty pictures in the world, but a golf course isn't designed until it has been shaped on the ground. In fact, I don't consider that a golf course is designed until it's built.

ECONOMICS AND SCHEDULING

Briefly, let me mention the issues of economics and scheduling. In any project, staying on schedule and on budget are important design considerations. Don't let anyone suggest they're not. I suppose I'm very aware of these factors because of my own background in the business. When I started with my Uncle George, we were designing and building courses as a turnkey operation for a single, all-inclusive price.

The twelfth at Wade Hampton in North Carolina (top right) is a short par four set beneath the sheer, white face of Chimney Top Rock, a dominant natural feature that was used as a backdrop on several holes. The par three eighth at The Virginian (bottom right) plays past a natural spring that emerges here after traveling a thousand yards underground, providing the principal hazard feature and interest of the hole.

I worked in the field and saw to it that the job got done. (The last thing Uncle George said before he left the site each day was, "Remember to work until dark.") I have a first-hand understanding of what it means to deal with the uncertainties of the weather, of subcontractors, and of people and machines who don't show up on time. A golf course that isn't finished on time can't open on time, and that may affect whether or not it's successful.

Without a sound economic and financial program, nothing works. With every new project, I want to know the client's program, timing, market, financing, schedule, and goals before deciding whether or not I'm interested. If we become involved, the first thing we do is prepare a month-by-month schedule from planning to permitting to commencement of construction to shaping to planting to grand opening. A schedule reflects milestones along the way, but also the planned opening of a golf

course. If the course is located in the hot California desert, for example, you don't want to have an opening in the middle of summer. Economics and schedule are as important to the end result of the golf course as the design details themselves.

FRAMING

As you probably have noticed while leafing through the photographs and captions in this book, the concept of framing is very much in our minds as we design golf holes. In my opinion, framing is a significant design consideration both for the long

A sliver of space among the boulders was an obvious natural frame for a par three, the eleventh at Estancia in Arizona (above left). Grass in front and a bunker on the left provide some margin for error on this all-or-nothing shot, but the hole is very short. The par four sixteenth at The Old North State Club in North Carolina (above right) is framed by Badin Lake, and is one of three spectacular finishing holes along the water.

range views golfers see and for the progression of individual shots and settings they encounter as they play a hole. This begins at the tee and follows golfers as they proceed along the fairway to the framing that's presented at the green. In addition, we try to find settings in which the hole is as attractive or dramatic looking back from green toward the tee as it is from tee to green.

When we compare historic "links" with typical American courses we see obvious differences in style and framing, due primarily to the differences in terrain and vegetation. Links courses, in general, are laid out on open ground that normally offers low vegetation and bunkers as distinguishing features. While often dramatic,

---

The par three fourth at Lake Nona in Orlando (above left) plays along the free-form edges of a lake to a green beyond a sandy beach that glides gently into the water. A wide bunker at the par four second at Sand Ridge in Ohio (above right) is a buffer between fairway and marsh on the right and helps frame the tee shot. Sand is a natural choice because the adjacent property is a working quarry that supplies sand to golf courses around the country.

even sensational, many links settings generally have few trees or strong elevations that would provide vertical frames for golf shots. Trees and elevations, on the other hand, have been features of American golf courses almost from the beginning because of the types of sites that were chosen.

Today we look for frames — trees, hedgerows, stone walls, creeks, natural contours, etc. — and if they aren't present, we create them. Safety is another reason for using vertical separations between holes because errant shots falling anywhere on the course are more of an issue nowadays than they have been in the past.

GREEN SETTINGS

In broad terms, we can say that green settings fall into three basic types — natural settings, man-made settings, and some combination of the two. I think most of us would feel that natural settings are the most appropriate and satisfying for golfers to play, and are the ones that most often provide us with dramatic golf. The truth is, though, that a certain amount of handiwork is required to render the most natural settings playable for golf.

The green at the sixteenth hole of the Mountain Course at The Vintage Club in Indian Wells, California, is such a setting, laid into a hillside at the base of Eisenhower Mountain. The placement of the green was almost obvious amid the rocks and steep slopes, but even here we embellished the hole with water features and rocks to complete the dramatic picture, and employed other measures to soften the natural setting so as to make it playable. On the other hand, the third green at Wade Hampton in Cashiers, North Carolina, is set into the base of a tall hill, and behind it is a waterfall that has been there for centuries. In this mountain setting, the green rests near the valley floor surrounded by steep elevations with mature evergreens and oaks marching up the slopes whose scale is brought into sharp focus by the cascading water. This is as good an example of a natural green setting as any.

In contrast to these, we often find it necessary to enhance green settings even

when we find a superior site, as was the case when designing the Seaside Course for Sea Island Golf Club in Georgia. Space for golf existed, although the land was rather flat and had very little in the way of discernible frames. So we sculpted a series of bunkers and rolling dunes into the sandy terrain, adding dune grasses and planting mature oaks at strategic spots to create settings and vertical frames for the greens on

The par four tenth on the Seaside Course at Sea Island, Georgia is framed by irregular dune shapes with oaks planted in strategic spots, acknowledging its setting on a natural linksland. The green is at the far left (just right of the tower) surrounded by billowing bunkers.

181

The par three eleventh at The Farm in Rocky Face, Georgia is set within a forest, playing down to a sloping ridge where the green offers the only level ground. The bunkers carved into the slope and the wide catching area on the right keep balls from bouncing into oblivion.

several interior holes on the front nine, and four holes on the back nine that range along the seaside and marsh. In choosing the sites for greens, we look first to do what is logical and what fits. It's never a good idea to force things upon nature, or to make something happen just because we have a bright idea. An extreme example might be trying to force a links style on a rolling, wooded piece of terrain, or anything that might be in conflict with the site.

A green is more than a putting surface; it's a complex structure that emerges out of the surrounding terrain. If we have done our job properly, the transition from terrain into the green structure looks natural. When we say we're shaping a green, we're really building a green complex that may include bunkers and mounds, slopes and contours that tie into the surface of the green. When we're building a greenside bunker, we start shaping its slopes and edges well away from the green itself so that the contours will look natural. We take into account all the contours of the putting surface in shaping a green complex so that even a two or three level green will seem to blend in with the contours of the surrounding terrain and appear to grow out of it.

We've learned a great deal about siting greens in recent years. In the past, golf designers didn't always pay attention to the long-term health of the green surface itself. Problems are created when greens are placed in spots where turfgrass has a hard time surviving. Potentially difficult growing conditions occur where dense, tall vegetation, or high elevation behind the green on the south and east sides keep turf in the shade. Sunlight and air circulation are essential for good, healthy turf and a quality putting surface. Without these, you might have little or no grass.

Some of the so-called classic golf courses suffer from green settings that have changed over the years, perhaps due to the growth of nearby trees that now create shade in which it is difficult to grow healthy turf. In some cases, this may not have been part of the original design but instead was the work of a later greens chairman or superintendent. Building a new bunker might cause a revolution within a club, but not many members would object to planting a tree or two, especially a small one, would they? But trees tend to grow.

Twenty or thirty years ago, we might have been inclined to fit a green into a natural setting that appealed to us without much concern for this sort of thing. Today we have a better understanding of the consequences of our routing plans and, as a result, where to place greens. We even pay attention to the issues of air circulation and sunlight, even during winter months in regions where bermuda grass becomes dormant during winter months and is overseeded with rye or other strains that survive in cool weather, because the bermuda base itself needs sufficient sunlight to survive. These considerations become very detailed but important parts of the planning process.

TEE PLACEMENT

Just as there are certain natural green settings, there are also natural settings to place tees. Most commonly, these occur at elevated spots where golfers can obtain a fine view of the hole as they prepare to drive. When golfers stand on the first tee at Cypress Point, their first look may not be drawn to the fairway or the green. Their gaze is probably pulled to the left, toward the ocean where the rocks, seals, and white ocean spray provide dramatic contrast to the golf holes. They probably say to themselves, as I do, "Isn't this a great setting? What a great course!"

A dramatic tee placement can offer as much satisfaction and pleasure as a beautiful green setting. The opening holes at Treetops in Michigan and Wade Hampton in North Carolina are examples where golfers experience sweeping views. So, too, is the seventeenth hole at The Quarry in La Quinta, California, where the tee is set on

---

The fifth at Victoria National in Indiana (top right) is laid into the irregular terrain left by an open pit mining operation, offering multiple, dramatic tee settings. The par three sixteenth at Hudson National in New York (bottom right) with its varied tee placements occupies a dramatic setting above the Hudson River, framed by the contrasting colors of fescue grasses and the dense tree cover behind the green.

184

the top of a ridge and provides golfers with a panoramic view of the faraway desert rim and of the fairway as it tumbles down the hill toward the green. Another beauty is at the thirteenth at Sand Ridge Golf Club outside Cleveland, one of the most natural tee settings I've encountered. (This hole is pictured on page 127.)

In a more practical vein, logic tells us that the teeing ground at a public or resort course will need to be larger than at a small, private course simply because more people will be playing the public course and more space is needed to rotate the tee markers. We also must take into account the traffic patterns between greens and tees on each course we design. This can often influence the placement and possibly the elevation of a tee, and certainly will affect where we put cart paths.

HAZARDS

Growing up in the game and observing my friends and weekend golfers play, I came to understand that golf would be more enjoyable for most people if cross hazards were kept to a minimum. As mentioned earlier, hazards that lie perpendicular to

---

The sixteenth on the Cypress Course at Bonita Bay East near Naples on the west coast of Florida is shaped in a gentle curve over and around natural wetlands on the site. The forward tees on this secluded par three offer easier angles around the hazards.

the lines of play add penalty shots to the scores of most golfers, and, to my way of

thinking, a golf course doesn't need a lot of penalty shots to be challenging or inter-

esting. That doesn't mean that we won't build a cross hazard when circumstances call

---

The par three seventeenth at The Quarry at La Quinta in the California desert plays over a lake to a
large green framed by bunkers. The high tee takes in a wide panorama of the finish, looking toward the clubhouse
and the mountains rising behind. We tend to find cross-hazards more acceptable toward the end of the round.

for it, but we do try to keep them to a minimum on our golf courses. For this reason, the majority of the creeks and ravines on our golf courses are designed parallel rather than perpendicular to the line of play. The same goes for bunkers; only rarely would I allow sand to cross the fairway.

The eleventh hole at Glen Oaks in West Des Moines was laid out in an open field, the fairway shaped from a flat plain into gently-undulating playing surfaces that pick up afternoon shadows from the man-made contours and clusters of vegetation. Fescues are used around the edges to set off the hole and direct golfers to playable areas. No hazards obstruct the direct line of play.

Another thing to avoid, if at all possible, is out-of-bounds markers on the interior of a golf course. That's really not acceptable today given the flexibility we have in choosing property. When out-of-bounds is unavoidable, it is better to place it on the left side rather than the right side of a hole. Of course this is not always possible, but it would be our preference because, as I've mentioned, the majority of golfers play on the right side of the golf course. The same idea applies to the clearing patterns used in establishing widths for the golf corridors. In the areas off the fairways, we are more concerned with clearing vegetation and undergrowth and creating spaces between trees on the right side of the hole than on the left. Fewer lost balls will result, which will have a favorable effect on the pace of play.

In certain locales, wind is golf's unseen hazard and should be taken into account in the design because of its effect on play. Courses along the ocean in the Carolinas or California are exposed to strong breezes, and so are golf courses in Texas and the off-shore islands. Wind is used as a design element in these locales, incorporated into the overall plan as are other kinds of hazards. Wind also influenced the design of some of our courses in the midwestern wind belt, including Flint Hills National in Wichita, Kansas; Karsten Creek in Stillwater, Oklahoma; and Glen Oaks in Des Moines, Iowa.

BUNKERS

My friend Jerry Pate, who has collaborated with us on several courses, told me once that bunkers are the most important feature on a golf course. If we look back to the origins of golf in Scotland, before there were trees on golf courses, said Jerry, the most significant strategic features on the great old golf courses were their bunkers. In the absence of other prominent features, they provided the principal interest in the game — where and how the bunkers were located, their size, the steepness of their banks, and the degree of skill required to escape from them.

Today bunkers serve many functions beyond those of simple hazards. Traditionally, they've been used to create shot values and suggest strategy playing a hole. In addition to these functions, bunkers have been commonly added as artistic features and to provide definition for fairway landing areas and green settings. Nowadays, they are used, as well, in coping with environmental issues, as buffer areas between golf holes and sensitive ecological areas. However, the use of bunkers as buffers in this way has grown increasingly common in our industry, even in our own work, and is an example of a treatment that is becoming a cliche. My concern is that too many golf holes are starting to have this look, and while it was a good solution at one time, we need to find other ways to handle this issue so that we can continue to provide golf courses marked by variety and interest.

Many golf courses have countless bunkers, into the hundreds, that are placed in areas for aesthetic reasons, as hazards, or to provide definition. At a site like Winged Foot in Mamaroneck, New York, and other places where the land was not dramatic, the designer — in this case A. W. Tillinghast — put drama into the golf course through the shapes and forms of his greens and bunkers. His upswept bunkers and elevated greens gave a distinctive look and playing character to the two courses he built there.

In the California desert, we modeled the bunkers for the Desert Course, the second of two courses we designed at The Vintage Club, after this Tillinghast style as a way to contrast it with the first one, the Mountain Course. In fact, we exaggerated the upswept faces that are such a characteristic of Tillinghast's bunkers at Winged Foot and at San Francisco Golf Club. If these bunkers had been designed in the east or southeast, however, they wouldn't be at all suitable because of the comparatively high level of rainfall in those regions. In the desert, which gets little rainfall, the steep slopes generally won't erode.

Over decades, golf architects have been pushing the tees back and moving bunkers forward to deal with the changes in golf, mainly the greater distances achieved by today's equipment. We rarely have a single goal in mind when placing bunkers, but instead relate it to the issue of variety. We always want to vary the design from one course to the next to avoid sameness. No matter how grand the shape or form of

PETER WONG

a bunker, we would not want to repeat it because that particular shape would soon get boring.

There is no reason why we can't design an infinite variety of bunker shapes, just as we look for an infinite variety of golf holes in our work. It has a lot to do with who is standing there with the paint can outlining the shape of a bunker, or who is running the backhoe when the bunker is excavated, or how it's finally edged. Even though we personally outline and flag every bunker on every golf course, we usually find some very artistic people on our crews who add a touch of originality to the process. Not all of the ideas for bunker shapes come from our staff, which is just fine.

The subtle textures of the Sonoran desert are captured at dusk at Grayhawk's Raptor Course in Scottsdale, Arizona, looking toward the McDowell Mountains across a wide lake that borders the approach to the eighteenth green. This sporty par five was played as a par four by Tiger and his friends in the Williams World Challenge.

191

I like the idea of using people who've never built a bunker before because it leads to new ideas and variety.

Hudson National runs along a tall bluff overlooking the Hudson River not far from New York City. Because of underlying rock formations and drainage issues, a site like this can require extensive adjustments in the field. Hudson National has become known, among other things, for the shapes and forms of its bunkers. Part of the reason for this is the dedication of the labor staff who had never hand-shaped bunkers before. Our staff outlined the bunkers, the elevations, and green shapes, and the crew followed behind to execute the detail. We encouraged them to express their ideas.

Tradition is a fine thing, and I believe in it, but we try not to be bound by how things have been done in the past. The designers on our staff are secure in their abilities and open-minded enough to look for new ideas as actively as I do. Our attitude is that anything we design — a hole, a green, a bunker, a golf environment — can always be done better. The reason the bunkers at Hudson National are so interesting is that the people doing the detail work had no preconceived notions, and had a great attitude about tackling the job. They cared about the work, and wanted to do it right.

To me, attitude is the number one factor in life. Almost all the people I've interviewed and hired over the years were chosen because of their attitudes, not their experience or education. With a good attitude and an open mind, I believe a person can do anything.

EVOLUTION OF GOLF COURSE CONSTRUCTION COSTS: 1960–1999

This chart shows the changes in scope and cost of work required to produce "state-of-the-art" golf courses in each decade

ITEM	1960's	1970's	1980's	1990's
Cost per Hole	$10,000 - $20,000/hole	$30,000 - $60,000/hole	$70,000 - $200,000/hole	$200,000 - $400,000/hole
Cost per Course	$190,000 - $380,000	$540,000 - $1,080,000	$2 - $4 million	$3.8 - $7.6 million★
Erosion Control	None	$0 - $50,000	$50,000-$300,000	$100,000-$500,000 average Maybe more on sensitive sites
Earthwork	Minimal	100,000 - 200,000 cu.yd.	300,000 cu.yd. plus	350,000 - 1 million cu.yd. plus
Cost per Course	$50,000-$100,000	$100,000 - $300,000	$350,000 - $750,000	$500,000 - $1.5 million plus
Shaping	Greens, bunkers only	Add tees, mounds, cart paths	Add fairways, roughs Emphasis on shadows	Shape entire property
Cost per Hole (for Shaping)	$1,000	$3,000	$3,000 - $10,000 "Modern look" emerges	$10,000 - $20,000 Return to "classic" design
Irrigation	Greens, tees	Greens, tees, fairways	Double row	Wall-to-wall or target play areas
Type of System	Manual	Minimal automatic $300,000 plus	Central controller $500,000	Computer control $1.2 million+/-
	100-200 sprinklers	200-600 sprinklers	500-800 sprinklers	1,000-1,500 sprinklers
Greens Construction	Push-up topsoil Little drainage $.25 - $.50/s.f.	U.S.G.A. specs introduced More drains $1.00 - $1.50/s.f.	U.S.G.A. specs become standard $1.80 - $3.00/s.f.	Underground blower/vacuum systems introduced $3.00 - $4.00/s.f.
Cost per Course	$35,000 - $70,000	$140,000 - $210,000	$270,000 - $420,000	$420,000 - $560,000
Grassing	Seed or sprigs: no sod	1-4 Ac sod allowance	4 - 20 Ac sod allowance New grasses developed	20-100 Ac sod per course Improved grasses, new bents, fast greens
Cost per Acre	$100-$200	$400 - $600	$500 - $850	$850 - $2,000 seeding/sprigging Sod cost: $12,500 per Ac
Landscaping	Minimal	Tees, greens, surrounds	Formal plan/entire course	Instant maturity
Typical Costs	$5,000 - $10,000	$25,000 - $100,000	$100,000 - $500,000	$500,000 - $1.6 million plus★
Permits	What are those?	Clearing & earthwork	Complex wetlands laws passed	Good luck! Hire lots of consultants
Environmental Impact	N/A	Endangered species laws passed	Approvals take 9-12 mos.	Approvals may never be granted on sensitive sites
Maintenance Complex	Use existing structures (example: barns)	Covered vehicle storage	Multiple structures to meet EPA & OSHA requirements	Expanded structures and new regulations EPA, OSHA, ADA★★
Cost	$ minimal	$150,000	$200,000 - $350,000/course	$350,000 - $800,000/course
Course Maintenance Costs per Year	4 - 8 staff members Tractor mowing $50,000 - $100,000	5 - 10 staff members 7- to 9-gang mowers $150,000 - $300,000	10 - 22 staff members 5-gang mowers $300,000 - $850,000	15 - 40 staff members★★★ Triplex mowers $750,000 - $1.2 million

★ Substantial increases have occurred on unique sites

★★ Key: cu.yd. = cubic yard; s.f. = square feet; Ac = acre; EPA = Environmental Protection Agency; OSHA = Occupational Safety & Health Act; ADA = American Disabilities Act. ★★★ Irrigation Specialists, Pesticide Technician, Equipment Operators

GOLF COURSE DESIGN PROCESS

Program Development
- Style and type of course
- Residential, commercial, corporate
- Private, resort, daily fee, municipal

Client Involvement

Design Guidelines
- Target market
- Playability
- Flexibility
- Memorability
- Walkability

- Budget
- Schedule
- Interest
- Variety
- Aesthetic qualities

- Federal, state, local constraints

Site Analysis
- Topography
- Soils
- Vegetation
- Water quality
- Hydrology
- Climatology

- Environmental sensitivies

- Vehicular and utility access

Preliminary Golf Routing Plans
- Accurate boundaries and elevations
- Schematic layouts
- Amenity relationships
- Open space system

Conceptual Land Use Plan

Client Approval   Preliminary Permit Process

Final Golf Course Routing Plans
- Tees, greens, bunkers and fairways, cartpaths
- Water features, lakes, creeks
- Practice facility
- Maintenance facility
- Clubhouse and parking
- Shelters and bridges

Permit Process   **Client Approval**   Cost Estimate

Golf Course Contract Drawings
- Construction schedule
- Utilities
- Erosion control
- Staking
- Clearing
- Earthwork
- Drainage
- Shaping-Contouring
- Irrigation
- Landscape
- Circulation
- Grassing
- Details

Permit Process

Bidding Procedure

Initiate Construction

Client Approval   Budget

Utilities

Complete Construction

Maturation of Golf Course

Open for Play

GOLF COURSE CONSTRUCTION PROCESS

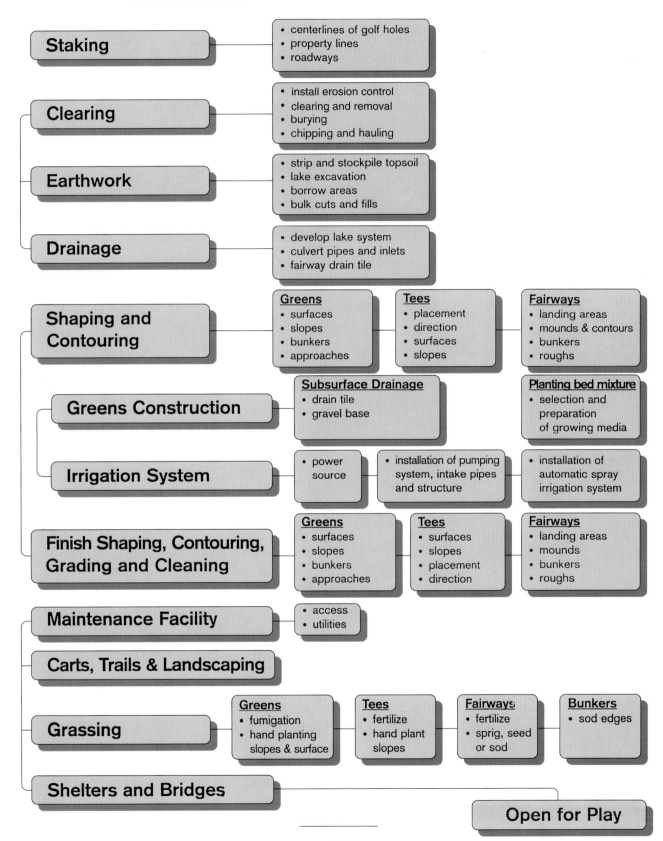

Staking
- centerlines of golf holes
- property lines
- roadways

Clearing
- install erosion control
- clearing and removal
- burying
- chipping and hauling

Earthwork
- strip and stockpile topsoil
- lake excavation
- borrow areas
- bulk cuts and fills

Drainage
- develop lake system
- culvert pipes and inlets
- fairway drain tile

Shaping and Contouring

Greens
- surfaces
- slopes
- bunkers
- approaches

Tees
- placement
- direction
- surfaces
- slopes

Fairways
- landing areas
- mounds & contours
- bunkers
- roughs

Greens Construction

Subsurface Drainage
- drain tile
- gravel base

Planting bed mixture
- selection and preparation of growing media

Irrigation System
- power source
- installation of pumping system, intake pipes and structure
- installation of automatic spray irrigation system

Finish Shaping, Contouring, Grading and Cleaning

Greens
- surfaces
- slopes
- bunkers
- approaches

Tees
- surfaces
- slopes
- placement
- direction

Fairways
- landing areas
- mounds
- bunkers
- roughs

Maintenance Facility
- access
- utilities

Carts, Trails & Landscaping

Grassing

Greens
- fumigation
- hand planting slopes & surface

Tees
- fertilize
- hand plant slopes

Fairways
- fertilize
- sprig, seed or sod

Bunkers
- sod edges

Shelters and Bridges

Open for Play

THE GOLF COURSE DESIGNS OF TOM FAZIO

Alabama

    Old Overton Club, Vestavia Hills (1993)

Arizona

    The Estancia Club, Scottsdale (1996)

    Grayhawk Golf Club, Raptor Course, Scottsdale (1996)

    Ventana Canyon Golf & Racquet Club, Canyon Course, Tucson (1984)

    Ventana Canyon Golf & Racquet Club, Mountain Course, Tucson (1987)

California

    The Canyons at Bighorn, Palm Desert (1999)

    Oak Creek Golf Club, Irvine (1996)

    The Meadows, Del Mar (2000)

    The Quarry at La Quinta (1996)

    Pelican Hill Golf Club, The Ocean South Course, Newport Beach (1991)

    Pelican Hill Golf Club, The Ocean North Course, Newport Beach (1993)

    The Preserve at Santa Lucia, Carmel Valley (2000)

    The Vintage Club, Mountain Course, Indian Wells (1980)

    The Vintage Club, Desert Course, Indian Wells (1983)

Canada

    The National Golf Club of Canada, Woodbridge (1974)*

Colorado

    Maroon Creek Club, Aspen (1996)

    The Club at Cordillera, Valley Course, Edwards (1997)

Florida

    Bayou Club, Largo (1991)

    Black Diamond Ranch, Quarry Course, Lecanto (1987)

Black Diamond Ranch, Ranch Course, Lecanto (1997)

Bluewater Bay, Niceville (1982 & 1986)

Bonita Bay East, Cypress Course, Bonita Springs (1997)

Bonita Bay East, Sabal Course, Bonita Springs (1998)

Emerald Dunes Golf Course, West Palm Beach (1990)

Gateway Club, Fort Myers (1988)

Golden Eagle Country Club, Tallahassee (1986)

Hammock Dunes Golf Club, Palm Coast (1989)

Hunter's Green Golf Club, Tampa (1989)

Johns Island Club, West Course, Vero Beach (1988)

Jonathan's Landing Golf Club, Jupiter (1978)

Jonathan's Landing at Old Trail, Jupiter (1986)

Jupiter Hills Club, Hills Course, Tequesta (1970)*

Jupiter Hills Club, Village Course, Tequesta (1978)*

Lake Nona Club, Orlando (1985)

The Legacy Club at Alaqua Lakes, Longwood (1998)

Long Point Club, Amelia Island Plantation (1986)

Mariner Sands Golf Club, Stuart (1980)

Osprey Ridge at Disney World, Orlando (1992)

Pablo Creek Club, Jacksonville (1996)

Pelican's Nest, Bonita Springs (1985)

PGA National Resort & Spa, Haig Course, Palm Beach Gardens (1979)

PGA National Resort & Spa, Champion Course, Palm Beach Gardens (1980)

PGA National Resort & Spa, Squire Course, Palm Beach Gardens (1980)

PGA Golf Club at The Reserve, North Course, Port St. Lucie (1996)

PGA Golf Club at The Reserve, South Course, Port St. Lucie (1996)

Riverbend Club, Tequesta (1971)

Summerfield Champions Country Club, Stuart (1994)

Windstar Country Club, Naples (1982)

World Woods Golf Club, Pine Barrens Course, Brooksville (1993)

World Woods Golf Club, Rolling Oaks Course, Brooksville (1993)

Georgia

Cherokee Town & Country Club, Atlanta (Rev. 1998)

Deer Creek at The Landings, Savannah (1991)

Eagle's Landing Country Club, Stockbridge (1988)

The Georgian Resort, Frog Course, Villa Rica (1999)

Reynolds National, Reynolds Plantation, Greensboro (1997)

Sea Island Golf Club, Seaside Course, St. Simons Island (Rev. 2000)

St. Ives Country Club, Duluth (1989)

The Farm Golf Club, Rocky Face (1988)

White Columns Golf Club, Alpharetta (1995)

Illinois

Butler National Golf Club, Oak Brook (1972)*

Conway Farms Golf Club, Lake Forest (1991)

Stonebridge Country Club, Aurora (1989)

Indiana

Victoria National Golf Club, Newburgh (1998)

Iowa

Glen Oaks Country Club, West Des Moines (1994)

Kansas

Flint Hills National Golf Club, Andover (1997)

Hallbrook Country Club, Leawood (1988)

Maryland

Caves Valley Golf Club, Owings Mills (1991)

Congressional Country Club, Fourth Nine, Bethesda (1976)*

Massachusetts

Wollaston Golf Club, Milton (1975)*

Michigan

Treetops North Resort, Fazio Course, Gaylord (1992)

Minnesota

Spring Hill Golf Club, Orono (1999)

Mississippi

Dancing Rabbit Golf Club, Azaleas Course, Philadelphia (1997)

Dancing Rabbit Golf Club, Oaks Course, Philadelphia (1998)

Missouri

Branson Creek, Branson (1999)

Missouri Bluffs Golf Club, Chesterfield (1995)

Montana

The Stock Farm Club, Hamilton (1999)

Iron Horse Club, Whitefish (2000)

Nevada

Edgewood Tahoe Golf Course, Lake Tahoe (1967)*

Primm Valley, Lakes Course, Primm (1997)

Primm Valley, Desert Course, Primm (1998)

Shadow Creek, Las Vegas (1990)

New Jersey

Galloway National Golf Club, Galloway Township 1995)

Pine Valley Short Course, Pine Valley (1992)

New York

Hudson National Golf Club, Croton-on-Hudson (1996)

Oyster Bay Golf Club, Long Island (1986)

North Carolina

Champion Hills Golf Club, Hendersonville (1991)

Eagle Point Golf Club, Wilmington (2000)

Forest Creek Golf Club, Pinehurst (1996)

The New Finley Golf Course, Chapel Hill (1999)

Old North State Club, Uwharrie Point (1992)

Pinehurst # 6, Pinehurst (1976)*

Pinehurst # 8, Pinehurst (1996)

Pinehurst # 4, Pinehurst (2000)

Porters Neck Plantation & Country Club, Wilmington (1991)

Treyburn Country Club, Durham (1988)

Wade Hampton Golf Club, Cashiers (1987)

Ohio

Sand Ridge Golf Club, Chardon (1988)

Saw Mill Creek Club, Sandusky (1974)*

Oklahoma

Golf Club of Oklahoma, Broken Arrow (1982)

Karsten Creek Golf Club, Stillwater (1994)

Pennsylvania

Hartefeld National Golf Course, Avondale (1995)

Philadelphia Country Club, Centennial Nine, Philadelphia (1991)

South Carolina

Barefoot Landing, North Myrtle Beach (1999)

Belfair, West Course, Bluffton (1995)

Belfair, East Course, Bluffton (1999)

The Cliffs at Keowee Vinyards, Pickens County (2000)

Country Club of Callawassie, Callawassie Island (1984)

Cotton Dike Golf Club, Dataw Island (1984)

Kiawah Island Club, The River Course, Kiawah Island (1995)

Moss Creek Plantation, Hilton Head (1978)

Osprey Point, Kiawah Island (1986)

Palmetto Dunes, Fazio Course, Hilton Head (1973)

Thornblade Club, Greenville (1989)

TPC at Myrtle Beach (1998)

Wachesaw Plantation Club, Pawley's Island (1984)

Wild Dunes Resort, Links Course, Isle of Palms (1979)

Wild Dunes Resort, Harbor Course, Isle of Palms (1985)

The Country Club at Woodcreek Farms, Columbia (1998)

Tennessee

The Golf Club of Tennessee, Kingston Springs (1991)

Texas

Barton Creek Resort & Country Club, Fazio Foothills Course, Austin (1985)

Barton Creek Resort & Country Club, Fazio Canyons Course, Austin (1999)

Champions Golf Club, Jackrabbit Course, Houston (1964, Rev. 2000)*

Virginia

Bayville Golf Club, Virginia Beach (1997)

Lowes Island Club, Cascades Course, Sterling (1992)

Two Rivers Country Club at Governor's Land, Williamsburg (1992)

The Virginian Golf Club, Bristol (1993)

* In collaboration with George Fazio

ACKNOWLEDGEMENTS

Senior Design Associates

Andy Banfield

Jan Beljan

Blake Bickford

Lou Capelli

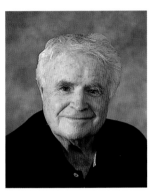

Charlie Feeley

Tom Griswold

Steve Masiak

Tom Marzolf

Kevin Sutherland

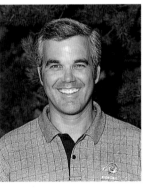

Dennis Wise

The ten individuals pictured above are Senior Design Associates of the Fazio golf course design firm. They join with me in thanking the other men and women of our staff who work with and support them. All are valued colleagues whose dedication and commitment to our projects has been a fundamental component of the firm's success.

◆   ◆   ◆

The concept for this book grew out of conversations with an old acquaintance, Cal Brown, a former writer and editor with *Golf Digest* who is now a freelance author and book producer. Cal assisted in the writing and editing of *Golf Course Designs* and was responsible for the book's development. In addition, I want to acknowledge the valuable help on this project of Beau Welling, a senior executive of our firm.

ACKNOWLEDGEMENTS

Principal photographers for this book are John and Jeannine Henebry, the brother-sister team based in La Quinta, California. Their work covered many months and many thousands of miles, and is much appreciated. In addition, several fine photographers generously contributed photographs to this project for the benefit of the Tom Fazio Children's Charity Fund, for which we extend our sincere thanks. They are:

Dick Durrance II, Drinker/Durrance Graphics, Carbondale, Colorado.

Mike Klemme/Golfoto, Enid, Oklahoma.

Peter Wong, Peter Wong Photography, Saint Paul, Minnesota.

David S. Soliday, Yemassee, South Carolina.

Russell Kirk, Blue Bell, Pennsylvania.

Evan Schiller, Port Chester, New York.

Stephen Szurlej, Port St. Lucie, Florida.

Credits accompany each of their photographs in the book. All other photographs are by John and Jeannine Henebry.

Most importantly, I thank my wife, Susan, and our six children for their love, patience, and understanding, particularly during the unavoidable absences over the years.

Finally, I want to acknowledge with sincere thanks the many fine golf course builders and contractors who have worked closely with us and with our clients.

INDEX